ALWAYS BE QUALIFYING

MEDDIC / MEDDPICC

By Darius Lahoutifard

Edition 5, July 2020

ISBN: 978-0-9892957-6-5

Table of Content

|

EDITORIAL REVIEWS & QUOTES

*"PTC achieved success thanks to the combination of a remarkable product and a talented and productive sales organization. In order to scale our go-to-market capacity, we needed to institutionalize and codify the sales best practices developed by the early team, so that new hires could rapidly ramp to full productivity. That's what led our sales leaders to develop the MEDDIC methodology. I am delighted to see the book on that methodology published. **ALWAYS BE QUALIFYING** is easy to read and to apply. It's sharp and to-the-point, just as MEDDIC itself. It's relevant now more than ever. I highly recommend it to any sales team in technology."*

- **Steven C. Walske**

Steve is renowned for building one of the most impressive enterprise software sales-driven organizations in the world, PTC, where MEDDIC was born. As CEO, Walske took PTC from founding to over $1 billion in revenue. Under his leadership, PTC had 40 consecutive quarters of increasing revenues and profits as a public company. His disciplined, methodical practice is now emulated globally. He now serves on the board of several prominent Silicon Valley companies including Synopsys (NASDAQ: SNPS), Medallia and Platfora.

He was previously Chairman at Bladelogic (acquired by BMC Software) and Endeca Technologies (acquired by Oracle). He advises VC-backed companies on sales processes and growth strategies for optimal revenue growth.

"Technology? SaaS? Private Equity? Accelerated Growth? MEDDICC is the gold standard for world class sales professionals and leaders. I have deployed MEDDICC in multiple companies as a CRO/CSO – it is an extremely simple, yet comprehensive qualifying tool to rapidly get to the bottom line and uncover gaps. It is also incredibly flexible – motoring through an entire list of deals or diving deep into each one – the framework supports a tailored approach to sales leader intent. Darius's persuasive text, with real world examples provide a foundation and set off best practices ready for sales professional/leader use. I highly recommend the book, Always Be Qualifying, to anyone in sales."

- **Scott Rudy**

Scott is currently Chief Sales Officer at Paycor ; He was an early and successive sales leader at PTC for over 10 years.

"Salesmanship is not an art. It's a structured process. MEDDIC is easy to understand and provides a common language for any company with the aim to build a

professional sales organization. ALWAYS BE QUALIFYING is easy to read and provides a very good structure to the understanding of MEDDIC. The challenges of bringing a product to the market and delivering relevant forecasts are more relevant than ever. ALWAYS BE QUALIFYING will help you understand how to better qualify opportunities, drive sales to closure and reduce risk in your forecast."

- **Göran Malmberg**

Göran is currently Group CEO/President of Mentice AB and Chairman /President of Mentice Inc. Mentice (STO: MNTC) is the world leader in software and hardware simulation solutions for endovascular therapies. Göran was one of the initial sales leaders at PTC who contributed to the early stage growth of the company as well as building the starting blocks of the organization, including MEDDIC sales methodology.

"In the best of times, selling complex enterprise software is an all-in team-based effort; many a times, it's even a 24/7/365 competitive engagement cycle with frequent changes across multiple key decision making constituents and parameters.

Faced with dynamics as such, it's critical for sales teams to constantly and continuously gather both account and opportunity intelligence, analyze it and strategize to make updates and/or revisions to win playbooks. To do so, you need a proven, structured and easy-to-operationalize Sales Qualification Methodology.

MEDDIC delivers; the qualification workflow and critical gates are laid out enabling both in-the-field execution and coaching/mentoring. And, the MEDDIC workflow is logical and can easily be an overlay on most companies' sales stages, entry & exit criteria. Lastly, MEDDIC is also a great qualification process for (big) deal reviews & inspections, and provides a great, factual learning experience for the expanded sales team.

This is an easy read, and if you are heeding the guidance and advice herein, you and your teams will reap the benefits.

Jump in!"

- **Kris Thyregod**

Kris is currently Vice-President & General Manager EMEA at Silver Peak where the book's author helped implementing MEDDIC globally. Kris has worked in technology for more than 20 years, previously serving in sales and marketing leadership positions at Riverbed, CA Technologies, Dell/EMC and IBM. Mr. Thyregod is a graduate of the Copenhagen Business School and Henley Management College with advanced degrees in organization, strategy and business administration.

"ALWAYS BE QUALIFYING is an easy read with no fluff. After reading this book, the sellers and their managers can surmount their challenges once they learn about successful

*and unsuccessful qualifications. I really enjoyed the WHY
and the HOW of MEDDIC. By the end of this book, sellers and
leaders learn how to close deals with no discounts in a timely
manner."*

- **Ramin Elahi**

Sales Enablement training Manager, Infineon Technologies &
Adjunct Faculty, University of California SC Extension

---

*"With the tremendous impact sales teams have on a
company's top and bottom line, it is critical that the quota
carrying professional can ramp up quickly, disqualify
opportunities not likely to close, and relentlessly focus on
qualifying the opportunities that will exceed their goals.
Darius Lahoutifard's Always Be Qualifying crystallizes the
techniques and mindset a top enterprise seller needs to
achieve these objectives. This book is not filled with academic
theories, but rather, it arms the seller with the highly
practical sales qualification methodology and techniques
known as MEDDIC, which Mr. Lahoutifard helped shape
while he was an early sales leader at PTC. He emphasizes the
need for sellers to continuously qualify opportunities
throughout the sales cycle, to stop wasting time on dead-end
deals, and focus on those that deserve their attention. It's a
methodology that shifts the urgency onto the buyer so the
compelling event is not the sellers need to close a deal, but the
buyer's need to avoid missed revenue, missed cost savings, or
reduction of risk. Always Be Qualifying also highlights the*

unexpected benefit MEDDIC has on improved team spirit and cohesiveness because the MEDDIC methodology not only improves sales performance, it creates a common language and understanding across the entire selling team."

- **Kevin Matsushita**

Kevin is Head of Partnerships and Alliances at MindTickle, a technology leader in sales readiness & sales enablement platform & software for improving seller effectiveness and increasing revenue.

PREFACE

WHY THIS BOOK?

In the past few years, companies large and small have called on me to get help with their non-performing sales team. Described symptoms are different from one company to another. Some suffer from shortages in revenue. Others complain about unreliable forecasts, with deals slipping constantly from one quarter to another before being lost or even abandoned a few quarters later. Some CEOs notice unproductive sales teams with an unusual high number of non-quota-carrying people needed in the sales force, hitting the bottom line hard. I notice that all these symptoms are related to the same illness: inability to qualify.

Since most sales teams put in place organizations including SDR (Sales Development Representatives) or BDR (Business Development Representatives) who qualify leads for Account Managers, there is a wrong unstated assumption, widely spread, that once a lead is qualified, the inside sales or field sales will have to work on them until they are won or lost. Ongoing qualification is often the issue. Qualification is not a binary step of the sales process. Qualification is a mindset and a habit to apply all along the sales process, from the first call to closing. This book covers both the **Why** and the **How** of sales qualification.

I was an early sales leader at PTC where the MEDDIC methodology took shape. I am also the founder of MEDDIC Academy, the first platform to bring the qualification methodology online. This book describes the M.E.D.D.I.C. (also known as MEDDPICC) sales methodology in depth. This is not a book of theories, research, or academic concepts, but it is pure execution techniques with practical recipes. At a high level, MEDDIC is a checklist that helps sales professionals to reveal the gaps in an opportunity and to execute properly to fill those gaps and close the deal or drop it early. This book is a great complement to the training and workshops that we deliver online and in-person, globally.

WHO NEEDS TO READ THIS BOOK?

Enterprise sellers may look healthy, be in great shape, be fun to interact with, and show amazing forecasts at the beginning of the quarter. But sometimes, despite the great look, they find reasons why their deals don't close on time.

If you or your team members are experiencing any of the following symptoms, you need to drop everything and get an in-depth education on MEDDIC/MEDDPICC now.

1. Your prospect claims they no longer have the budget to purchase.

Sounds familiar? A deal is in the "commit" forecast for the second quarter in a row, and the prospect sends you an email saying, "Unfortunately we'll need to postpone the project to next year, since the budget allocated for this project is no longer available." You consider this a legitimate case where nothing can be done. If there's no budget, then they can't buy, right? So you take it off the forecast and move it to the pipeline for next year. You love working on long-term deals and building the pipeline for the future.

2. Opportunities on your forecast get delayed from one quarter to another.

You are in a deal review session with your sales manager and share the news that a prospect sent you an email saying, "Unfortunately we'll need to postpone the project to next year. This project is not a priority right now." You dig in with the prospect and find out that their CRM (Customer Relationship Management) project is taking all their IT team's resources. You understand that you can't do anything. If there are no resources allocated, then they can't run a POC (Proof of Concept), etc., right? So you take it off the forecast and move it to the pipeline until the prospect is ready to act. You are excited that you are building your next year pipeline.

3. Your so-called Champion explains why the Economic Buyer never meets with vendors.

Your sales manager wanted you to obtain a meeting with the EB. You asked your "champion." He/she replied that he/she can meet with the sales manager, but that the EB never meets with vendors. Since it appears to be a rule at this company, you share the information with your sales manager and respectfully explain it's not going to be possible at this account on your forecast. You enjoy the transparent communication with your sales manager.

4. Your prospect changes Decision Criteria, reducing your chances to win.

You are selling a SaaS (Software as a Service) CRM solution, competing with an on-premises offering. Although the prospect was only looking for SaaS architectures at the beginning, they inform you that they have changed their mind, and they now consider on-premises solutions can also be used. They state that on-premises architecture presents some benefits in terms of security. You think that's a legitimate observation and, since they are still considering the SaaS model as acceptable, then there is no reason to object or worry. You are happy that the prospect is moving forward with the project. You put the champagne in the fridge.

5. You learn that you have to run another POC before getting the order.

After running the POC, the prospect mentions some aspects have been omitted in the POC and that you need to run another one. You talk to your Sales Engineer and Consultants and prepare them for another POC. You feel good, since it will make your case stronger when it will be shown to the decision makers. You are more confident about this deal in your forecast.

6. Prospects' Buyer or Legal Executive refuses to sign your terms & conditions.

You have been working on this deal for a year now. We are a week away from the end of the fiscal year, and you are checking emails, waiting for your PO. That's when you receive a call from your "champion" informing you that they are preparing a PO with their General Procurement Terms that they use with all vendors and that they won't be signing your license agreement. This symptom is usually accompanied with high fever and above-normal blood pressure.

7. Prospects Buyer asks for a significant discount because they are a big name.

They say they have the choice between two possible vendors and that the other vendor has made an attractive offer. Your solution now requires a 40% discount to be considered for purchase. You are excited to have brought the deal this far and to hopefully be the one who will sign this "big name." The discount appears high to you, but, hey, if your sales management wants the deal they have to accept it, no? You invite your significant other to dinner to celebrate the progress with the customer.

8. You believe saying YES to every request from your prospect is the key to success.

You are proud of your business background and have been raised with the saying, "The customer is always right." So, if the prospect or customer is asking for something that your company can't deliver, then it's not your fault. You feel like a very positive and contributing member of the company and decide to send the prospect's requests to marketing and a few more people in management as something the company needs to solve in order to address your market. You also expect congratulations in return.

9. You have taken the free "Introduction to MEDDIC" course at MEDDIC Academy and consider that you learned MEDDIC.

You learned all about MEDDIC. It's done. Over! You considered it was just another sales methodology. You are proud to know what MEDDIC stands for. It's not that bad, but most of it doesn't apply to your business anyway. Now let's get back to the good old habits.

If you are an individual contributor and are experiencing the above symptoms or similar ones you need to read this book, at a minimum.

If you are a sales manager and see these symptoms in your team members, make sure you have a plan to implement MEDDIC / MEDDPICC in your organization.

CHAPTER *ONE*

QUALIFYING IS CLOSING

You have probably heard the famous line "Always Be Closing" from the movie "Glengarry Glen Ross" starring Alec Baldwin, Al Pacino, Jack Lemmon, and Kevin Spacey. These words, spoken by the character played by Alec Baldwin, hardly represented a new idea when they were quoted in the movie. More than being just a slogan in a movie, "Always Be Closing" is a concept, a motivational phrase, a philosophy, according to which any good salesman must be in a constant state of closing sales. And the fact that the acronym is ABC, it's a perfect way to assume that it's the ABC of sales.

That type of sales is no longer tolerated among more educated buyers or in more strategic Enterprise type of sales. With the democratization of the Internet in the early 2000s, information became accessible to buyers who became more informed and took away the drive from the sellers. A seller who is "always closing" with no real value added to the buyer appears pushy and is disliked and ignored. Moreover, it's not a smart way to sell anyway, since there are situations where you need to take a lot of effort only to realize that the buyer will never buy. Worse is even when the buyer ends up buying due to a high pressure from the seller, not because they had evidence of a match between their needs and the product. They'll regret it, try to cancel the sale, or return the product. In the end, at best they'll be an unhappy client, a counter-reference, destroying the seller's reputation.

Closing is obviously a key step of sales because, no matter how well you perform elsewhere, if you don't close the client, then you have wasted your time. But as this sample sales process shows, there are a lot of steps before closing. If you miss some of these steps, and sometimes even if you miss only one of these steps, you can miss the sale.

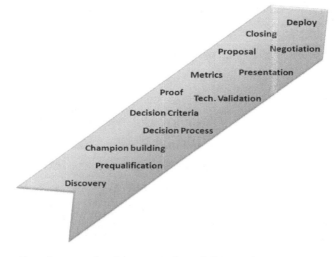

In other words, there are a lot of things that may go wrong during a sales process that may lead to the delay of the deal beyond your end of quarter (i.e. forecasted as commitment in the quarter). Or they may even lead to the loss of the deal. You may get outsold by a competitor who had a stronger internal support than you. Or you may have underestimated the importance of some features you don't offer. Or the decision makers may consider that there are other investments with a higher priority than yours. I can go on with the list of all the things that may go wrong so that, no matter how great you are as a closer, you will still miss the deal.

Let's take two Account Executives, Megan and Aaron. On paper they have very similar backgrounds: both have bachelors from well ranked universities, and both have two years of sales experience. Megan comes to us from Oracle, where she was a Sales Development Rep. Aaron has a very similar profile, joining us from Salesforce. Both are new to the job, in their first quarter. Aaron appears to be very energetic with quite a high level of activities, such as calls and demos; he also spends more time in the office, while Megan seems to leave often earlier than Aaron. Some say Aaron looks like Alec Baldwin, the "Always Be Closing" guy.

Around the middle of the quarter, Megan's forecast has 10 lines with only three committed deals totaling $300k ARR (Annual Recurring Revenue). Seven more deals are in best case, totaling an additional $700k. Aaron has a more impressive forecast with 10 deals in the commit column totaling $1M.

One month later, that is two weeks prior to the end of the quarter, on their updated forecast, Megan has $200k done (two of the committed deals got booked) and still the same $300k committed forecast for the quarter, with some more deals in best case. The 3rd committed deal is still there in the forecast, although not closed yet. But Aaron's forecast is already half what it was one month earlier, that is $500k. Moreover he has not closed any of his deals yet. He explains that in one case the client told him they are delaying the purchase. In another case the project was cancelled since the budget was allocated to another project. One client needs more time to run the POC (Proof of Concept) and Aaron feels strongly that the project is delayed by only a couple weeks but won't come in this quarter. For the last deal in the forecast, the client is hit by a massive layoff. But Aaron is very confident that this time his forecast is solid. He feels more upbeat than ever, committing to $500k.

The quarter ends. Megan scores $400k. All three deals are signed plus one of the best case deals. Aaron books two deals for $200k total. Even three of those he had hoped to book just two weeks before the end of the quarter didn't close, but they were not lost. The great closer in Aaron manages to bring in two contracts on the last day of the quarter. The sales director sighs!

Lack of luck? Bad territory? Just a bad quarter? What is the difference between Megan's clients and Aaron's?

Do you think Megan's clients never have layoffs or any delay in their projects? Of course they do.

Do you think Megan's clients never need more time to run POCs? Of course they do. It happens all the time, right? So why did Megan have a better judgment than Aaron on her deals?

The difference is the QUALIFICATION. It's the assessment of how solid each deal is. It is the ability to remove those pink glasses and evaluate a deal's solidity.

Megan focused on highly qualified prospects. She had the same number of deals as Aaron, but she considered only three of them strong enough to meet her qualification criteria, to be considered in her "committed" forecast. She didn't waste time on deals that she knew would not close.

Aaron was not qualifying his deals, and was working hard to close each and every prospect he could possibly talk to. Despite putting more hours into his work, and despite being a great closer with a likeable personality, he didn't make it.

> *Successful sellers are those who spend their time with prospects who will end up buying.*

It is common sense, isn't it? Still, too many sales people fail to execute qualification. Sellers need to objectively and constantly assess their prospects in order to know if they can be qualified and if they will be closed before a given date.

One short but deep set of simple (but not easy) questions you should ask yourself to qualify an opportunity is the following three famous whys:

Why anything?

Why us?

Why now?

Why anything? Why would the prospect consider buying anything at all? This is about the "I" of MEDDIC as we'll see later.

Why us? Why would the customer award this contract to us? This puts us in the customer shoes and tries to look objectively the reasons why the main decision makers will trust us. We will see later that this is related to several elements of MEDDIC such as the "M", the "DC" and the "C" of MEDDIC.

Why now? Why wouldn't the customer delay the decision? What creates the urgency that is pushing the customer to buy now, instead of sometime in the future? We will see later that this relates to the "compelling event" as we cover the "E" and the "DP" of MEDDIC.

Here's my definition of Sales Qualification:

> ***Sales Qualification is the act of assessing prospects, as quickly as possible to determine whether they will buy from us and become successful users of our products and services within a given timeframe, for a given amount.***

Now when Aaron learns MEDDPICC and understands the value of qualification, and he applies it, his numbers will explode, thanks to his high level of activities, focused on the right opportunities.

One hard thing for Aaron will be to stop wasting time with a prospect that does not meet the qualification criteria. But it's necessary to cut some useless activities so that he can focus on more qualified deals and spend his time bridging the gaps in those accounts, taking them to closing.

CHAPTER *TWO*

INTRODUCTION TO MEDDIC/MEDDPICC

MEDDIC, or its longer variant MEDDPICC, is a recognized sales methodology that is widely used in technology and other enterprise sales context, especially when the sales cycle is rather long and complex. It helps vendors to:

- Increase revenue thanks to higher sales productivity
- Improve forecast accuracy thanks to a higher level of intelligence into the prospect's decision-making process
- Reduce costs thanks to savings of presales resources and efforts
- Increase profits thanks to higher revenue AND lower costs
- Create common language in the sales force, leading to more cohesive team spirits

Senior sales leaders who come to discover MEDDPICC usually describe it as a sharp and practical methodology in comparison to other methodologies, which are abstract or theoretical and not practical enough.

What does MEDDIC stand for?

MEDDIC is the world's most renowned Sales Qualification Methodology, applicable to any Enterprise Sales Process, which is rather complex. The definition of MEDDIC is the acronym it represents, composed of six elements. They represent the MEDDIC checklist as described below:

METRICS: Measure the potential gain leading to the economic benefit of your solution vs. competition.

ECONOMIC BUYER: Identify and meet the person who has the final word in releasing funds to make a purchase.

DECISION PROCESS: Know and influence the process as defined by the client to make purchase decision.

DECISION CRITERIA: Know and influence the criteria as defined by the client to make purchase decision.

IDENTIFY PAIN: Identify and analyze the pains that require your solution to be relieved.

CHAMPION: Identify, qualify, develop, and test your champion, the person who sells inside the account on your behalf.

In a nutshell, MEDDIC tells you that if you do the above in any complex B2B sales opportunity, you win the sale. If you can't achieve these elements, then avoid spending time on this opportunity for now, and focus on those you can, or prospect more and bring in new opportunities in the pipeline.

How about MEDDICC (with a 2nd C)?

MEDDIC has a few variants. MEDDICC, with two Cs in the acronym, adds "Competition." Obviously, knowing your competition and strategizing your account plan based on who you are competing with is absolutely a must. But is MEDDIC without that second C incomplete? Or does it mean you are ignoring the competition? Absolutely not! As a matter of fact, "Competition" is inherently present in every action you engage in the account.

In fact, some MEDDIC elements, such as "Metrics and Decision Criteria," would not make sense if you don't refer to competition. Adding "Competition" to your checklist would be like adding the "Purchase Order": hey, make sure not to forget to ask for the PO! But if you feel more comfortable explicitly naming the competition and pausing or reflecting on your strategy, that's perfectly fine. That's why MEDDICC became a variant of MEDDIC.

Where do we cover the Competition?

Metrics are, by definition, a comparative measure of benefits, obviously compared to the competition, which could be the incumbent system or the non-decision. Metrics force the seller to consider competition. During MEDDIC courses at MEDDIC Academy, one of the key concepts that you learn is how to link a set of decision criteria to a vendor, whether it's one of your competitors or your company. Decision Criteria is also another element that forces sellers to consider competition. Are the decision criteria in your favor or in favor of one of your competitors? Is the playing field tilted?

Now, as mentioned before, if you think you may forget the competition, and if you feel better referring to MEDDIC as MEDDICC with a second C, then you are very welcome to do so. It definitely does not hurt to emphasize that we need to know the competition, know what their weaknesses and strengths are, and, most importantly, know who their champion is.

Definition of MEDDPICC

MEDDPICC emphasizes the paper process. Sellers need to understand the process through which a purchase request has to go inside that company for such a deal and execute accordingly. Anyone with experience in complex enterprise sales knows that interactions with the legal department or purchasing team could be a nightmare if they are under-estimated. Especially since these interactions are at the end of the sales cycle and the deadline for the PO may be compromised, whether it is the end of quarter for the vendor or the implementation expectations for the client. These issues take time to resolve, often leading to a delay in the purchase order. It is absolutely necessary for the Account Executive to understand the "paper process" and to anticipate the issues. For instance you can avoid those issues by sharing your company's standard contract or TOS (Terms Of Services) earlier in the process.

Some would say that the paper (purchasing and legal) process is part of the decision process, just like the technical approval process and business approval process. Well, the difference is that often the champion knows very well the technical and the business process all the way to the approval by the Economic Buyer. But they don't always know the paper process themselves. That's why it does make sense to add it to the checklist, to make sure we understand it, and that our champion understands it. That's why we adopt a proactive approach with the legal and purchasing departments, to avoid any delay in the PO.

How did all this start?

MEDDIC & MEDDPICC are the result of the Sales and Qualification techniques developed at PTC (Parametric Technology Corp.). PTC is a software company known for having built one of the strongest sales cultures in the context of Enterprise Software (now SaaS). The company had over 40 quarters of continuous growth during the 90s. The initial Global Sales Management team at PTC, that I was a part of, developed different elements of MEDDIC in the field. We used to meet in Boston every quarter to share our notes and experiences. Our challenge was to grow as fast as possible before being copied by the competition. We had to execute well and quickly. In sales management, if you want to grow fast, you should be able to hire well and quickly, and to train the new hires well and quickly so that they ramp up quickly and generate revenue. So, we had to be able not only to identify our key to success, but also be able to articulate it in a sharp and easy way so that the new hires could learn quickly and execute. That was what we shared in the sales management meetings every quarter. Later, PTC training managers at the headquarters in Boston leveraged these best practices from the field. They put them together into a formal practice course for new hires and gave it a name: MEDDIC!

In my case, I was hired to run France, which was one of the most strategic regions for the company and was where two of my predecessors had already failed because the region was where we had our toughest competition, Dassault Systemes. I took PTC Southern Europe from $4M to $27M in three years, beating Dassault in their own fiefdom. Dassault is a French company that had over $4B revenue in 2019. As anecdotal note, Dassault was, and still is, the only vendor that PTC never managed to beat globally (in terms of revenue, market share, head count, etc.). What my team did in Southern Europe was all done by rigorously applying MEDDIC, even though the acronym was not used at that time yet.

MEDDIC is a Qualification Methodology

Designed for complex Business-to-business sales, MEDDPICC helps sellers to qualify whether a prospect will close in a given time period, usually a quarter. And if it does not, it tells us what needs to be done so that the deal does close in the defined timeframe.

This methodology takes the effort away from fostering dead-end leads and helps sellers to focus more on identifying and nurturing the opportunities that have a higher chance of making a sale. As previously mentioned, very often the problem is not with a salesperson's skills in negotiating or closing a sale but rather on his/her judgment to properly assess if a deal is going to close or not and, consequently, their decision whether that prospect is worth their time in the short term. This is commonly called SALES QUALIFICATION, as described in the previous chapter.

The fact is, you could have a stellar sales pitch and amazing sales skills, but if you don't have the right judgment and assessment of the deal's strengths and weaknesses, then you will not be able to properly direct your efforts. Every sales process needs to begin with first understanding your prospect, understanding their needs, and qualifying them for their likeliness to make a purchase before spending any more time and effort on them. Even if you make sure that the customer is in your target market, they may still have reasons for not being a closable opportunity for this quarter.

MEDDPICC brings this concept into a foolproof methodic approach that many big and small companies have successfully applied.

It is important to know that MEDDIC is not a sales process; it is a qualification methodology, which can be used with any process that determines whether or not a customer is a qualified buyer that you should invest your time and effort into. It focuses on identifying the key elements or criteria of a customer to determine whether or not the customer will end up buying and if you have the solutions that they seek.

As mentioned in Chapter One, instead of considering the ABC of sales, Always Be Closing, MEDDIC is built with the mindset of ABQ: Always Be Qualifying. This is an important shift and effective way of understanding your customers, and even people in general, to effectively communicate with them and assess their needs and desires. It helps you to assess what you can offer; this is true in personal relationships as well. It is like learning their language so that you can decide if you can or want to speak it.

MEDDIC isn't a process on its own, but rather it is a method that works well with any sales process that you may already be working with. So instead of replacing your current sales process, MEDDIC will integrate into it to make it more effective. MEDDIC can help identify the loopholes in your sales process. It pushes you to ask yourself:

"Where am I now?"

You need to begin by identifying where exactly you are in your sales process with a specific customer. How good is your interaction with your customers?

We can use MEDDIC together with a process that is currently productive with the customer, with one that the customer decides to take you through, or with one that your company chooses to use.

Important Characteristics of MEDDIC

The following are some important characteristics of MEDDIC that make it so unique and effective.

It is a short checklist: Once you learn this methodology, all you will need to do is check these six or eight elements whenever you are trying to make a sale. This is universal because it works with every business model and structure. These elements don't need to be altered in any way.

This isn't a conditional methodology, making it very easy to implement.

It is activity based

This means that the analysis and assessment of a deal within the framework of MEDDIC will lead to a certain number of action items by the sellers. They will have to do something to uncover the unknown or to change things in the account.

It reveals gaps

MEDDIC helps you identify gaps between what you have already accomplished in the accounts and what elements you still need to take care of.

It is self-assessing

You don't need to seek help from your manager, mentor, coach, or an expert in the industry to understand this methodology. You can easily assess and identify the different elements of this process by yourself.

It brings a common language to your team

MEDDIC helps to create a common language among the sales team. For instance, when you talk about identifying pain, your sales engineer, your consultant, your customer service rep, and your manager all know what you are referring to. You and your team will no longer have different answers or confusion regarding these key elements of a sale. You all will be on the same page regarding whom the Economic Buyer (EB) is, whom the champions are, and what the metrics should look like.

Your Current Sales Process

What is your sales process? The good thing about MEDDIC is that it will work alongside your sales process to further strengthen your chances of successfully closing a deal, or it will help you to see the red flags early and decide to drop it or to reduce efforts on it.

Most processes have a similar format. They usually start with prospecting and discovering; at this point, the MEDDIC questions will be general. The next step in the sales process is usually the scoping and go-no-go. This is where the MEDDIC questions become more specific. And then the last phases usually highlight elements like Validation, Proposal, and Closing; this is where you will need to confirm your MEDDIC questions as you get close to signing the contract.

The MEDDIC methodology is highly effective not only in identifying wins and losses, but also the NO Decisions.

MEDDIC helps both the reps and the sales managers. From the reps perspective, MEDDIC provides a checklist that helps identify the key elements to successfully closing a sale.

As a sales representative, you really need to understand if you've answered all the required questions to drive the opportunity towards closing. You also need to be able to identify all the missing elements, as well as have a good understanding of what your next step needs to be once you have all the information that you require. MEDDIC helps us to successfully guide and track these questions.

MEDDIC helps sales managers develop a common language amongst their team members. MEDDIC can help identify the missing elements, outline the next activity, and forecast the stage that the opportunity is at. It also helps sales managers identify where you need to go next or what you need to do to move further ahead in the sales process. It also helps set short term goals for easier implementation and tracking.

MEDDIC Helps You Avoid Useless Activities

Here is what a sales process without the MEDDIC methodology implemented at the right times looks like: you initiate contact with a customer, and you spend your time and effort on developing resources (these could be the POC, the pilot, the custom demo, a reference call or IT review). Once you have all the elements ready, you run them through with the economic buyer, and they tell you that the solutions don't resonate well with the company, that they don't promise to deliver the quantifiable results that they had expected (metrics), or that they are just out of their budget. You are left hanging dry after all those efforts and investments because you hadn't really taken the necessary steps to ensure that your solution and the customer's 'pain' were indeed a good fit.

Now, most salespeople will tell you that this is just part and parcel of the business that you need to be prepared for dead-ends like these. But MEDDIC helps identify a dead-end much earlier in the sales process. It stops you in your tracks before you invest too much time and effort on an opportunity that doesn't QUALIFY or deserve that time and effort because it won't close.

With the implementation of MEDDIC, the same sales process looks like this: you initiate contact with a customer, and then you run it through the elements of MEDDIC in order to identify the pain and the key person who is responsible for making decisions. It then provides quantifiable outcomes of your solution and then takes the next step only if the customer responds positively to your qualification process. You then only invest time and effort on customers that will close.

Chapter *THREE*

METRICS

What is a Metric?

This is the first component of the MEDDIC process, and it focuses on identifying and explaining why a buyer will consider your solution. It is the documentation of the measured performance and economic impact that your solution creates for existing customers or that it will create for prospects in comparison to their existing situation or to the competition's solution.

The main objective of a metric is to turn subjective gains into objective measurable gains. Sure, a customer is happy with their purchase. But how happy are they really? And how does that happiness translate into quantified business gains? What did the business achieve with the help of your solution? A metric helps to outline solutions in a measurable form that greatly helps in the decision-making process.

Good METRICS should have the following characteristics:

- M: Measurable— The outcome of your products/services should be measurable
- E: Everyday Language— The language should be simple
- T: Tells a Story— Your metric should explain how it can help a business by telling a story
- R: Result of an "After-State" Comparison— It should be able to compare what the situation was before the integration of your solution and what was it like AFTER it.
- I: Impacts Economics— How it impacts the economy of business, whether it increases revenue or decreases costs.
- C: Champion Supported and/or Authored— The champion should support the measured metrics.

Examples of METRICS

Here's a real example of Metrics expressed as a statement by a MEDDIC Academy customer.

Twelve months after implementing our sales methodology, company XYZ noticed monthly revenue had increased by 200%, compared to the previous year.

You can notice that it is presented as a **measured** gain, in **every-day language** understandable by anyone, that it **tells a story**, includes a **before-after comparison**, leads to an **economic impact,** and is supposedly supported by the **champion**.

Here's another example, satisfying the same list of characteristics:

> *By installing a new vending machine in the lobby of their manufacturing site, company XYZ, noticed time saving for employees leading to an increase of productivity, which translated into $10k additional monthly profit.*

Once again, the statement is presented in easy to understand language, a far cry from specialized financial analysis language, by telling a story that quantifies the benefits compared to a previous situation and leads to an economic impact.

How to Collect Data

Your gains need to be measurable. Let's say you are selling a vending machine. You ask your customers if they are happy with the purchase. They then tell you that they are very happy. But this shouldn't be a good enough answer because it isn't measurable. You cannot calculate the effectiveness of your solution just by the fact that a customer is happy with it or that they are going to be happy with it. You need to inquire further. You need to know exactly what the 'gains' are. How did your solution add value to your customer? And so you inquire further:

"How exactly did my solution help you?"

"It offered snacks on the spot for my employees."

The idea is to turn subjective gains into objective gains. You want to know exactly how a solution helped a customer. So you probe until you get measurable responses.

"But what's the gain? Why did you invest in a vending machine when you had a cafeteria? What if you had not installed the vending machine?"

"The employees would have to go all the way up to the third floor to the cafeteria for a chocolate bar or even a water bottle. This would mean more traffic at the elevators, which would mean a slower commute for employees coming back and forth for work. It would also mean longer tea breaks. And the employees wouldn't be too happy having to wait for the elevators and commuting for that long to get a simple snack."

You then help the customer quantify those outcomes further. So, if a total of 50 employees each take five minutes longer than usual and takes two breaks a day, it adds up to more than eight hours of wasted work time during the day. Next, add in the slower commute for employees waiting for elevators that are busy elsewhere. Say an employee has to wait three minutes longer each day at the elevator, which adds up to an additional two and a half hours of wasted work time. This all adds up to 10 hours and 30 minutes of greater productivity each day because of installing a vending machine.

Now, these are quantifiable results. Assuming an average hourly rate of $40 for employees at this location, we are talking about a benefit valued at approximately $10,000 per month. Would you have guessed that a vending machine could make such a large impact on the company's profits? Well, there are ways to make it happen!

It is important to know that no economic buyer or business would invest in a solution until they are completely sure how the solution would impact their business. Without a measurable sales pitch, you are missing out on an important tool for leveraging your sales.

Sources of Metrics

There are two main sources for collecting metrics: your existing customers and your prospects.

It is easier to collect data from your existing customers as they have already purchased and benefitted from your solutions. Existing customers help you learn more about the real economic impacts because they know their business.

Try speaking with your existing customers and ask them for stories of how your solution helped them. These stories can help you to convey confidence and conviction to prospective buyers.

So how do you collect data from a potential customer? The fact is that the prospect will come to you because they have a problem that they would like you to solve. You need to first identify their pain during your discussions. You need to know exactly what is it that they are trying to achieve. Are they trying to mitigate risk? Is there some goals and objectives that they are trying to achieve? Are they trying to reduce costs or increase revenue?

You need to know their pain before you can offer metrics as a part of the solution. You need to know where they are at the moment and where they expect to be once they implement the solution. So, there is a metric involved in trying to understand the pain also. Try to quantify the gain they expect to receive.

Another way to collect metrics is during demonstrations. With enough experience, you know some of the key differentiating concepts or features that lead to great METRICS for your other customers. Immediately after presenting each of these concepts or demonstrating these features, pause for a few seconds and ask the client what they think about what you just presented or showed. Start with an open question.

"How do you like this feature/concept?"

If you have the right understanding of the PAIN and of their INDUSTRY, and if you are talking to the right people in this account, there is a high chance they'll say:

"It's great!"

Remember: we are talking about a few key features that you know are considered killer apps by most of your existing clients. So, if a similar client is not finding them to be great, it means you probably presented it the wrong way or maybe they were sleeping. Restart that part of the demo.

Then ask another open question and help them develop their thought process.

Ask "what is great?" or "what do you like about it?"

Then drive the conversation down towards metrics collection.

- "How much time do you think you'll save thanks to this feature?"
- "How many more projects do you think you'll be able to handle in the same timeframe with this feature?"
- "How much do you think your team productivity will increase thanks to just this feature alone?"

If your product has just a few differentiating features, and, after presenting each of them, you pause and collect some metrics, even though at this stage they need further validation, then at the end of the presentation you can help them assess more general metrics in time saving, productivity increases, or other gains.

The key is that it's not you who are promising any metrics. It comes from them. You just help them express the gains and measure them.

There are a lot of benefits in doing so. One benefit is that now when you mention METRICS to other customers, you are credible. They'll understand and believe you. You create trust.

Another benefit is that you can tell which metrics resonate better with the client. The same exact product functionality can be a source of savings or as an engine to grow revenue. It can enable time saving or accelerate growth.

By starting with collecting small metrics, you also set the tone for the scope of the Proof of Concept (POC), if necessary. It then takes less effort to explain why the POC needs to include certain tasks or elements; those tasks will require those key features and help leverage them.

This is one of the most effective ways to use metrics on prospects. It enables them to predict the possible 'gains' for themselves. This method is obviously not as strong as collecting from someone who has already implemented your solutions, but it is a great way for the customer to measure the rate of success for themselves and to start building a quantified case leading to a great ROI (Return on Investment).

Metrics and the Economic Impact

There are two primary types of economic impacts of a solution: the revenue and cost. But there is a lesser implemented impact also: mitigating risk. We can calculate these three impacts, also known as the R-C-R, with the help of metrics to further influence a buyer's decision. For instance, when speaking to a prospect, you could investigate how your solution can positively influence these main factors that contribute to the economic impact.

Revenue: Look for metrics with which your solution can positively influence revenue; for example, x% increase in existing revenue streams.

Decreasing Costs: Ways your solution can reduce costs of management, costs of duplicates, cost of many day-to-day operations, etc. Be specific with how much your solution could save. So rather than saying, " this will save time", you should provide a definite metric like "our solution has cut down service calls time by 20% at customer XYZ."

Risk: This is not an exact number and is only effective at the top management level. For instance, your solution may be a software that makes a business's product compliant with a standard in their industry, such as the GDPR in Europe (General Data Protection Regulation). Or it could be an HR software that mitigates the risk of losing talent or reduces legal risks.

A good example of a metric that we mentioned earlier is this amazing testimonial by one of our clients, Rajeev Agrawal, CEO of Innoviti.When asked to make a statement for our website, he replied:

"We implemented some of these (MEDDIC) and the result is that 12 months out, our monthly revenue is three times what it was 12 months back."

This testimonial is an example of how the implementation of a solution added value to the business by outlining definite metrics of the outcomes. As a CEO, or someone in a position of authority like Rajeev, it is predictable for them to look at numbers before making important decisions. However, MEDDIC can be effectively used in day-to-day life as well, and anyone can make it an important component of their decision-making process. It offers clarity and direction for various aspects of an individual's life.

How to Use Metrics to Attract Prospects

Metrics are not only useful during your interactions with the prospects in the sales process, but they are a strong tool that you can integrate into your marketing agenda. Highlighting important metrics on your website and through your marketing channels can help attract prospects who are looking for similar outcomes as those provided by your solution.

Ideally, you should have a collection of data that highlights the gains, in the form of metrics, for various customers and in different verticals and various industries. You could simply have a collection of one-liner metrics, like Rajeev's testimonial, for each of your customers. Having these one-liners helps strengthen your sales pitch when speaking to prospects. So, all you'd need to do is find a metric from a business that is pretty similar to that of your prospects.

Asking Open-Ended Discovery Questions

These are questions that have no right or wrong answer and cannot be answered with a yes or no. You need to let the customer define the experience for you. Help the customer/buyer, as well as the seller, analyze the situation. Allow the customer/buyer to expand and give details. For examples:

T-H-E-D: This acronym stands for four types of popular questions.

"Tell me about ...?"

"How do you ...?"

"Explain to me ....?"

"Describe for me ....?"

Also, a lot of open-ended questions in discovery start with the word "how," such as "how do you currently do this...?"

Discovery questions don't lead to metrics, but they lead to identifying pains, which will help localize where you should collect metrics.

Where to Look for Metrics

The most challenging aspect, however, is to collect enough data to define those metrics. This happens by asking the right questions AT THE RIGHT TIME. Timing is essential. The following are some ways to obtain metrics at different steps of the process:

When Prospecting: This is when you and your prospects are just warming up. Be sure to keep it low key or a prospect might feel overwhelmed and intimidated. Ideally, you should try to identify their pain points and quantify them.

During Demos: As mentioned before, when, during or after a demo, a prospect is excited about killer apps or hot features that are your key differentiators, this is a great time to get metrics. Ask them what they think is great about it. What did they like about it? How do they believe your solution could help them or their business? What will be the gain provided by your solution?

As highlighted above, metrics are a key component for the success of a product/service purchased by a business. And, the earlier the sought-for metrics are integrated into the sales process, the higher the chance of success.

CHAPTER *FOUR*

ECONOMIC BUYER

There is a bit of confusion about the definition for Economic Buyer. That's because of the word 'buyer'; sometimes, the sales team considers the economic buyer to be someone with the title "buyer" who works in the procurement department. But, in reality, it is far from true: the economic buyer is rarely the actual buyer in the procurement department. One exception that comes to my mind is when the customer wants to buy procurement software.

The economic buyer is, in fact, the person with the authority to decide whether to purchase.

An economic buyer will be the ultimate authority in a company regarding their purchasing decisions. They usually have certain characteristics such as:

- They have discretionary use of funds and can create budgets or change the priority of the budgeted items
- They have veto power, which means that if everyone else on the group agrees to purchase from a specific vendor, the economic buyer can reject that decision

- They are in charge of the 'bottom-line.' In other words, they are equally concerned with increasing revenue and decreasing costs.

The economic buyer will expedite the entire process to assess whether due diligence was done to ensure all aspects of the solution were closely analyzed. They will also be the one who asks difficult questions such as 'how will solution impact the business?' Ideally, this is where your METRICS will come into the picture to convince the economic buyer of your solution.

The Typical Economic Buyer Titles

The title of an economic buyer varies depending on the size and the industry segment of the company. Typically an Economic Buyer will hold any of the following titles:

CEO: For smaller or midsized companies, the CEO is likely to be the economic buyer for any contract above $100,000 in a small business account.

CxO (CTO, CIO, CMO etc.): For larger companies, these could be any of the varying titles, depending on the solutions that you are offering. For instance, if you are offering a solution that could elevate a company's marketing strategy, then it will likely be the CMO.

VP/ Director of/ Head of: These position holders could also very well have discretionary access to funds in their domain of authority.

You don't necessarily have to guess who the economic buyer is. You could easily ask your champion to provide details about who the EB is and what their budget is. There is a fair chance that your champion would be aware of the budget allocated to a specific solution. You can then compare this to your other customer wins to see if, for similar size of clients and similar size of deals, the EB had the same title or not. We'll discuss this further detail.

How About the Director of Purchasing?

It is also important to know that the economic buyer would hardly ever be the Director of Purchasing. It can be confusing because they often pretend to be the economic buyer. They play this role to make you believe that they are responsible for making final decisions. However, their only goal is to improve the terms of the contract. Their job is to get the lowest price and the best terms from any given vendor. They will try to get discounts and make a better deal at their terms. They are NOT the decision-makers in the company.

Let's say you are selling a CRM software (Customer Relationship Management). A typical call from the purchasing department is a buyer or a purchasing manager calling you to say this: "Hi there! I (or we) have been given three possible vendors files by the sales operations team to purchase a new CRM application. You are one of the three lucky vendors. I am (or we are) going to make the final decision based on our negotiations with the three vendors. We need an updated proposal with your best ever offer with no regrets if we don't select you due to your high price or unfavorable terms."

This is usually a lie. The more realistic way things happen is that the Sales Operations team has most likely decided to purchase from vendor A, after having considered vendors A, B, C and D. They turn to the purchasing department and ask them to finalize the contract with vendor A. The purchasing department asks for the proposals of A, B, and C and pretends that no decision is made in order to negotiate the price and terms. If you are new to sales, you may believe the buyer's statement, get nervous, discount as much as possible, give them the best terms, and do all of that in vain. Either you are vendor A and, regardless of your discount, the buyer has to buy from you, or you are vendor B or C, and, no matter the amount of discount, they won't buy from you anyway. They just used you to get the best deal from vendor A.

"Why are things like this?" you may ask. Well, it's because we are talking about strategic products and services, based on real enterprise pains and driven by metrics that lead to serious economic impact. We are not talking about purchasing ballpoint pens and other office supplies. It's not the purchasing manager's job to choose the product that will make or break the company's profitability. They neither have the competence to evaluate most of these projects nor have been given that as a goal. In our example of purchasing CRM, the VP of Sales or CRO has their job attached to the choices they make for. It's serious matter. Why would they let purchasing make arbitrary decisions based on terms or the percentage of discount? Why would they care about paying a bit more or even a lot more, as long as they get a higher sales productivity that drastically increases their revenue and, as a consequence, leads to a better Return On Investment?

Another key point here is the implication of your champion. Before receiving that call from the buyer, your champion will alert you. He/she will tell you what exactly the context is and hopefully he/she will be in the call/meeting with the buyer.

In the example of a CRM purchase, the economic buyer is most likely the CRO. And hopefully your champion is VP of Sales Operations. The Economic Buyer is the one who holds the budget and gives instructions to the buyer

How do you find the EB?

Ideally, you ask your champion for this valuable information, as mentioned earlier. The champion may not always know this answer, but if you ask the right questions, they should be able to give you the right information. We'll see more about this when talking about developing champions. You want to ask: Who is the person who'll make the final economic decision for this purchase? If you don't have a champion yet with experience of your industry and with clients of this size, you should know the title of your EB and check who holds that role in the company. You can double check who made final decision for similar purchases. You need to confirm and double check that the EB is the EB by asking them when meeting them: "Who else will need to review this purchase decision other than you?" This is an additional way to see if the EB confirms our information. Finally, one other characteristic of the EB is that they usually have a Profit and Loss management role.

Operational vs. Functional Decision Maker

Another source of confusion is when two potential EBs are involved in a purchase. But there is always only one EB in any opportunity. For instance, CRO and CIO may both be involved when purchasing a CRM software. Or Head of HR and Head of IT may both be present for a HCM (Human Capital Management) software deal. This happens almost always for application software because the IT department is involved and has the investment, or the OpEx (operational expenditure) in their budget partially or totally, while the real benefit is for the operational department: sales in the case of

CRM and HR in the case of HCM. So the question is: in the case of a CRM purchase, "who is the EB?" Is it the CIO or the CRO? To answer the question, ask yourself these questions:

- If the CRO and the CIO have a strong disagreement about the choice of the CRM vendor and take it to a hypothetical arbitration, the CEO, who's arguments will prevail?
- Who will win the internal fight?

What-ever answer you get is the person who has the final decision in hand. Most of the time, it's the pain sufferer. Whoever has the pain is going to decide: that is the CRO for purchasing the CRM system and the Head of HR for a HCM system. They are usually, but not always, those who get the biggest benefit of the change and have the most relevant metrics. This can be true even if, which is often the case, the IT department holds the budget for the CRM system. Worse, the project manager who coordinates the CRM replacement project could be in the IT department and working somewhere under the CIO. That's why, in most cases, especially in large organizations, the CRO is the EB for a CRM replacement project. Head of HR could be the EB for an HCM replacement project. Operational managers are more often EBs than functional managers. Ironically, operational managers are less available, less accessible to vendors, and talk less than their functional peers.

Now there are exceptions to these rules. When the reason for replacing the CRM is technical (IT related) or due to integration issues or something related to support, the CIO is the one with the pain and usually acts as the EB. Even in this case, the CRO has the power of veto.

Another exception is the personality and the charisma of the EB. Sometimes some characters inside a company go beyond their titles.

Of course, in matrix organizations these decisions are supposed to be made in a harmonious way with good coordination, but the reality is that, when the project is strategic with big impacts due to metrics, with a large scope, and with aggressive competition pushing in different directions, the differences inside the company emerge, and you need to understand the power base and act accordingly.

How about "Executive Committees"?

They tell you that there is no one single EB, that the final decision is made by the board of directors or an executive committee. Believing in that is like believing that the EB can be the procurement director; it's naïve. That committee is composed of different people who will cast a vote. And that committee has a chairman. Your job as an account manager is to figure out who has the final word. In an extremely rare situation where the committee is hard to assess, then it possibly means that the CEO is your EB.

Tune Your Sales Pitch to the Right Frequency

You will need to be cautious about the way you communicate with different stakeholders of a company. Your sales pitch will vary depending on who you are speaking to. For instance, an individual contributor wouldn't be very interested in the costs or turnover of an application, but they may be rather interested in its application and ease of use. Similarly, the CEO will be more concerned about the bottom line or the metrics related to return on investment (ROI) for your product.

Your sales pitch needs to be at the right frequency when speaking to people in different positions in the same business. Not sure what this means? Let's divide an organization into three main categories: the individual contributors, the managers, and the CxO or CEO. You need to align your message depending on which of these categories you are speaking to. This applies to pretty much any company; you have the contributing task force, then you have the middle management, and then the CxO.

As is evident, every individual, based on their position in the company, has a different way of thinking; they are all at different wavelengths. And to meet that wavelength, you need to attune your frequency to match theirs'.

The Individual Contributors want to know **HOW**: They are most concerned with how a product works or how your solution will impact their day to day operations. So when you are speaking to these individuals, you need to focus more on how your solution works and how it can influence and/or enhance their tasks.

The Middle Management wants to know **WHAT**: These people are more concerned with the scope of what you are offering. What problem does the solution that you are offering solve?

The Economic Buyer or the Top Management wants to know **WHY**.

The EB is most concerned with why they should even bother considering any change to start with. Next, they want to know why they should talk with you. And, even if they have satisfying answers to the first two questions, they want to know the urgency of the subject. Why does this need to be done now and not next quarter or next year?

How to Align Metrics with Your Message

Many reps make the mistake of saving up all their metrics to share with the top management. Sure, they are the decision-makers, but they will be taking input from all across the board. Metrics serve a strong purpose in each of the sections of an organization. Hence, you need to focus on different metrics for different stakeholders.

For individual contributors, you want to focus on metrics related to how your solution can save time and increase performance. This is the area where they are most involved and, thus, would be most interested in knowing more about. For example, executing tasks twice as fast allows them to perform tasks in a shorter time and handle more tasks in the same period of time.

The executives and managers, on the other hand, will respond most to metrics involving cost and risk reduction as well as increased performance. The top management provides performance goals to the executives and managers that they need to meet; thus, this is the area that these people would be most interested in.

The top management will also be interested in metrics regarding cost and risk along with important metrics regarding revenue, market share, and even competition.

Taking the same example of features that enable faster execution, you will present the metrics as time reduction and cost savings when talking to the management. You can extend this to cost reduction of production or even labor savings. In most situations, you are providing a productivity tool to the client. It's up to the client to use it as a way to reduce costs and resources while maintaining sales capacity, or increasing capacity and ultimately sales, with the same level of available resources. You need to be cautious in the choice of examples of your metrics while talking to different people at the company.

The Meeting with the Economic Buyer

This is a key step that is often ignored. In the sales process that we discussed earlier, this meeting NEEDS to happen at the Go No Go level of the process. This will be the determining factor as to whether or not you should proceed with your sales process and keep the deal in your committed column of the forecast.

We want to meet with the EB, at least twice. In the early meeting with the EB, we want to learn, understand, and validate the six elements of MEDDIC (or the eight elements of MEDDPICC). That is, we need to observe the pain, the relevant metrics, before deciding on the change, the EB's role, the Decision Criteria, the steps of the technical validation, the Decision Process, the steps of the business validation, the timing, and the other things relevant to a given opportunity. Why buying anything? Why us? Why now? One great question to ask when meeting the EB is: "What needs to be done so that we meet again within x weeks to formalize our business relationship?" Once the decision process is explained to us by the EB, which usually includes the validation process (often in the form of a POC), we want to do some conditional closing; "... if we meet the success criteria of the POC, are we going to be your selected vendor?" Or at a minimum, "Can we schedule a meeting after the validation step (POC) to go over the results together?"

In the second meeting, typically after the technical validation, we want to review the technical validation and the metrics, confirm how the metrics translate into the economic gain, create and observe the urgency due to the economic loss of NOT having the solution in place, observe this compelling event, and push for closing.

The fact is if, in the first meeting, the Economic Buyer does not give you the green signal to proceed, any other efforts on your end would very much be wasted. So this meeting is crucial for successfully closing the deal later. You or your champion need to meet with the Economic Buyer BEFORE you engage in other costly efforts like the Proof of Concept, longer custom demos, reference meetings, and all the other efforts that require time and resources.

You or your champion need to be completely satisfied with this first meeting with the Economic Buyer before moving forward. This will be your qualification moment to move on to the next step of the MEDDIC methodology.

Most salespeople, especially those who have not been exposed to MEDDIC, wrongly consider only the second meeting with the EB, which happens only towards the closing. As mentioned before, this is wrong because, if you discover issues in that meeting, revealing that the deal will not close, it's too late to pull out and focus on other deals. YOU HAVE

FAILED YOUR QUALIFICATION AND THAT'S THE PRICE YOU PAY: LOSING A DEAL AFTER SPENDING A LOT OF EFFORT ON IT. It's common sense but not practiced by too many people in sales.

Now the fact that we meet with the EB early in the sales process does not mean we won't solicit the EB for the second meeting to execute closing. On the contrary, one of the key goals of the first meeting with the EB is to get our "return-ticket" as mentioned before. That is the agreement to meet again after the client has done their due diligence.

CHAPTER FIVE

DECISION CRITERIA

The third important consideration is the Decision Criteria. This is the 'shopping list' of a business. It is the outline that they draw to find the most suitable and cost-effective solution for their business. You need to understand what their criteria are to make your sales pitch most effective. The fact is that a company will have multiple choices, and they need to have set criteria to opt for a solution that best caters to their requirements. So while you may have a stellar product that outshines the competition by a fair margin, if it doesn't meet these criteria, then it isn't a viable option for the prospect. To make your solution relevant and ahead of your competition, you need to focus on the important factors that a prospect will consider during their decision-making process.

Most Decision Criteria address three critical aspects:

- Vendor/Partner Criteria
- Financial Justification
- Capability Validation

Vendor/Partner Criteria

Criteria in this category focus mainly on the vendor. A business could have specific criteria determining the specific characteristics that it is looking for in a vendor. This could be the size of the company, the geographic location, the longevity as to how long they have been in business, their shareholders, their financial profile, or their reviews.

As a seller, you need to understand the specific characteristics or qualifications that they are looking for when deciding on a vendor. Understanding these requirements will help you to better represent yourself. This may not exactly be a deal-breaker if you don't meet those specifications, but it can be a major influence in their decision if you don't pay attention to it.

The following are some important questions that an organization will likely inquire in this regard:

Is the vendor worthy of our consideration? This focuses on the company's profile. This could be through your website, your brochure, or simply an outlook of your company.

What is the company's financial strength? They'll look at whether it is a startup or if they have the capital to provide quality solutions.

Does the company have good references locally and in the industry? This will be the company's track record of satisfied customers. They would want to know what others who have opted for your solution are saying about you. Are they happy with their purchases? Have they successfully experienced the ROI that they had been promised or are expecting? What is their positioning compared to those of their competitors in terms of customer satisfaction?

What is their track record of success? Nobody wants to work with a company that hasn't been successfully able to deliver on their promises. They want to know if your claims are worth the money.

How long they have been in business? Do you even have the experience to provide specific solutions? The experience takes precedence over most other partner criteria because an organization wants to know whether your solutions or your capabilities are seasoned enough to be invested in.

Financial Justification

A business will most definitely have a predetermined price range for their solution before they go out shopping. They will also have a good idea of how much Return on Investment they are looking for. They would want justification that your solution could help them save a specific amount of money. You need to find out their Decision Criteria regarding the financial aspect before moving forward with the sales process.

The following are some important questions that a prospect will likely ask on the financial end before shortlisting you as a suitable candidate:

How is value delivered with the least risk? What will my company gain from this without exposing it to too many risks?

What financial impact will the system have on our business objectives? How will the solution be able to serve the business's objectives more efficiently?

What is the impact on cost? Is the solution able to successfully deliver the business's objectives?

What is the impact on lowering risk?

Capability Validation

This highlights the list of features that a business is looking for in a solution. Your product or service needs to tick all the boxes on this list to be a suitable solution. Sure, any additional features may give you an edge over the competitors, but if it doesn't meet all the requirements on this list, then all the other bells and whistles just wouldn't make the cut.

This is by far the most important aspect of the Decision Criteria since it directly addresses an organization's 'pain' or requirement for seeking a solution. The following are some specifications that a business may have on their checklist:

- List of Requirements
- List of nice-to-have or optional features
- Specific functionalities that will drive the outcome
- Ranking, scoring, weighting criteria tied to outcomes

Decision Criteria vs. Your Solution

This is a key function of sales in general. When you are meeting with a prospect, they will talk about their needs in a certain manner. They may not always be specific about what they are looking for, but they might start by giving you an outline of what they want. As a sales rep, it is your responsibility to read between the lines and to probe further as to exactly what they are seeking and whether your solution fulfills those requirements.

You need to ask the right questions, based on the information listed in the previous section, to seek clarity regarding the Decision Criteria of a prospect. You need to know exactly what features they are looking for, how soon they need the solution to be integrated, the type of vendor they are looking for, and the budget that they have allocated for it. Once you have all this information, you could then go on to tally it with your solution and see if it ticks all those boxes.

Your solution may not always match their requirements. There may be a few features that meet their Decision Criteria and others that may be missing. Similarly, there may be some 'additional' features in your solution that a prospect may not necessarily need or have highlighted during their briefing.

As a salesperson, it is your role to influence them and bend their expression of needs to your solution. In sales, you cannot change your product or your solution. You cannot go up to the development team or the manufacturer and say 'you know what, you need to fix this solution to better cater to a specific client;' you cannot do that! You can always provide feedback, and your engineering team will appreciate it, but that won't help you to close the deal. You must sell the solution as is, unless, of course, you offer custom solutions. You cannot be apologetic about the lack of features or functionalities of a solution. You need to sell the product off-the-shelf, and you better endorse it and love it. You need to focus on the features that align with a prospect's requirements and Decision Criteria as closely as possible. So that's why you need to influence the Decision Criteria in order to bend their criteria to match as closely as possible to your solution.

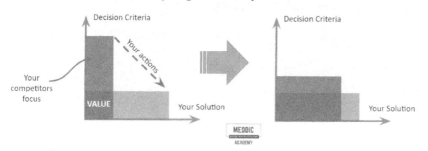

Another way to look at this is to tilt the playing field. You can tilt the field if you are early enough in the account. You could influence the way they express their needs so that your solution is the natural response to their needs. Your competition will then have to run uphill if they want to catch you, to either flatten the field by opposing those criteria or, worse, to reverse the playing field.

Photo credit: Dgrosso23 - Flickr - CC 1

Your competitor may have already played their cards and, with your experience and knowledge, you know that the competitor will also be trying to tilt the proverbial playing field. Your objective, at this point, should be to level out the playing field by looking for the loophole that your competitor has not been able to tap into.

The Value Triangle

The Value Triangle is a subset of the customer's Decision Criteria that we, as a vendor, satisfy and that our competition does not. The larger it is, the better the deal is qualified. Best sellers focus on it, enlarge it, make sure it's solid, review it often with the client, and, most importantly, leverage it.

First, we have the customer's expression of needs. We're presenting this in a triangle. Inside this triangle we have all the different elements of the Decision Criteria. As an example, let's imagine we are Google Cloud, selling G-Suite, and we're competing with Microsoft 365.

**CUSTOMER'S
DECISION CRITERIA**

**Customer's
expression of
needs and criteria
for decision**

The Decision Criteria may include requirements such as:

- Need for native cloud architecture
- Easy migration path from all our existing Microsoft Office data
- Advanced features for book publishing
- etc.

All these criteria are inside this first triangle. Then we have our own solution's characteristic, features, and benefits, also presented in a triangle, the darker, lower one on the left below.

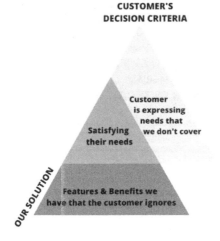

These two zones are overlapping. Usually it's almost impossible for them to match. Hopefully they are not too distant from each other.

When considering the overlap between the customer's expression of needs and our solution's characteristics, we notice three zones, as mentioned in the image above:

1. Criteria/requirements that we satisfy or cover.
2. Those that we don't cover or satisfy.
3. Features or benefits that we are proudly announcing to the market but the customer is not expressing any interest into them.

Now, of course, we are not alone on the market; we have competition, which can be another company offering products and services or can be the existing system or non-decision. Our competition, whoever or whatever they are, also has features and characteristics that they promote. When we look at the competition together with our solution and the customer's expression of Decision Criteria, we notice that there are seven different zones.

Analysis of The Decision Criteria Triangle

Let's go through each of these zones and analyze them.

The PARITY zone is composed of a series of needs or Decision Criteria, which are expressed by the customer that both us and the competition satisfy. Obvious and boring!

Next is the MARKET TRENDS zone. These are capabilities or characteristics that we offer as a vendor, as well as our competitor, but the customer is not asking for them. This happens sometimes when vendors develop new features that they think that the market is going to ask for or is asking for, and some customers, the majority of those who are not early adopters, are not yet asking for. Sometimes they don't care for a while. The best example is when the cloud architecture started to be known in early 2000. There were a lot of customers who were not interested.

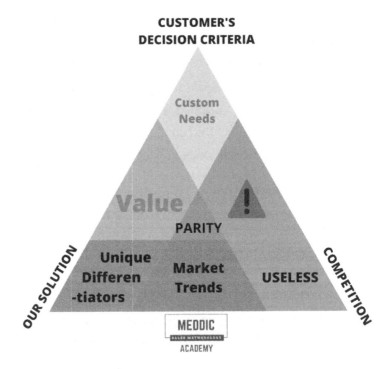

USELESS features are those that the competitor is bragging about that the customer is not interested in and that we don't offer either.

Our UNIQUE DIFFERENTIATORS represent a zone where we have some key strategic capabilities that the competition doesn't have but the customer is not asking for (yet).

At the top of these triangles resides CUSTOM NEEDS. Those are capabilities or Decision Criteria that the customer is expressing but neither us nor our competitor can satisfy. The customer may need to go through some custom developments to get them.

Most important zones

The last two zones are the most important ones. On the left we have a zone called the VALUE TRIANGLE. As mentioned at the beginning of this section, this zone is a series of Decision Criteria and capabilities or features that the customer is asking and that we can satisfy but our competitors cannot.

The DANGER zone, which is exactly the inverse of the VALUE but for the competitor, is where the customer is asking for some capabilities or criteria that we cannot satisfy but our competition can. That's the danger zone.

To win a deal, we need to flatten the playing field and even tilt it in our direction. We do that by leveraging the VALUE TRIANGLE, while shrinking the DANGER zone.

How to Act on Each Zone?

Now that we have identified and categorized these seven zones, let's see how to act on each of them.

PARITY & MARKET TRENDS

Don't waste time on these two zones, other than presenting your solution to make sure that the customer understands the parity on the criteria in this category and that they don't wrongly underscore your solution there. Always validate your assessment with the customer. Spending time and effort on parity features is working equally for yourself and your competitor. That's not the best use of your time.

USELESS

Unless the competitor manages to change them and bring them into the customer's expression of needs, you don't need to waste time on them. Remember, in just the same way you try to influence and change the Decision Criteria, an aggressive and smart rep at the competition, possibly trained with MEDDIC, will be trying to transform their USELESS zone into differentiators and into needed features.

UNIQUE DIFFERENTIATORS

You need to expand and enlarge the value of these features and show the client how they have helped other customers achieve metrics. Usually there is a reason those features are in your product or service. There is a high chance many customers are successfully using them. Ask yourself the question: Why isn't this customer asking for these features? Unless you have a very valid response to this question, you can help your customer revise the Decision Criteria to include your unique differentiators in their expression of needs.

VALUE

This zone should capture the most of your efforts and attention. You should expand, detail and leverage these criteria that the customer is asking for and that you offer and that your competitor is not. You need to make sure the customer fully understands and appreciates your offer and is conscious that you are the only one offering those. You also need to make sure that they stay in the Decision Criteria by reinforcing their importance, as seen with other customers, because your competitor will be working hard to try to remove them or to shrink their importance. The features in the VALUE zone should be omnipresent in your pitch. They should emerge in your presentations. They should be leveraged during the proof of concept. They should be refreshed by customer testimonials or reference checks. You should develop metrics related to these criteria.

DANGER

In opposition to the VALUE zone, you need to be conscious that the competitor, if smart and aggressive, is also focusing and leveraging the DANGER zone on par with your efforts in the VALUE zone. Remember, your VALUE zone is their DANGER zone and vice versa. How do you deal with that? Investigate that zone, assess it, and shrink it. Question the validity of those needs. Why does the customer express those needs? How crucial are they really? Since you have great customers with great metrics who are successfully using your solution without these features, then why are they so crucial? How can the customer live without them? Help the customer imagine the final solution without these features. Of course it's possible since you have customers doing so.

CUSTOM NEEDS

There is no general rule for this zone. Some companies love doing custom work and making offers here. Some don't, and they either bring in a partner or try to shrink those needs or satisfy them with their off-the-shelf features. There is one technique that was notoriously and successfully used by PTC in the past, that I am going to share here. We used to call it "commitment." It was used only with large strategic accounts. The idea was that if a large strategic account is asking for something we don't have, and our competitor does not have it either, then it will become a VALUE feature if we develop it as an off-the-shelf feature in a future release. Who better than a large strategic customer can define the specifications of what needs to be developed? Based on these ideas, we would connect the champion at the account with our product line managers and do our best to include those features in the road map. Of course the devil is in the detail: you don't condition the contract to the delivery of the feature, and the commitment should be on a "best effort" basis, but it's a great technique involving product marketing, aligning future developments with key customer needs while helping to close deals. That's why the action is called COMITTMENT for the custom needs zone.

The picture below summarizes your action plans on each zone.

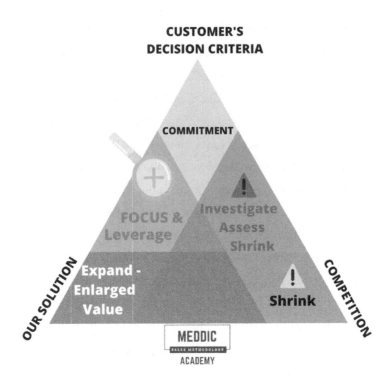

Chapter *SIX*

Decision & Paper Process

The Decision Process is mainly the internal process of a prospect for signing up on a solution. It is the step by step procedure that they usually follow to make a decision. Technically, it has nothing to do with your solution, but it has everything to do with how you make the sale. You should know about their buying process to better understand and implement your selling process.

You could directly ask them about their process for making a decision. There are usually two components to the Decision Process: the validation and the approval. Validation focuses on the technical and functional aspects, while approval focuses on the financial, administrative, legal, and commercial aspects.

It is important to document this process in writing so that you can refer to it during your own sales process. You can also create a visual representation of the process with the help of a timeline to better keep track of it. This timeline should begin with the initiation or the current time and span up until the prospect makes the purchase.

At the top of the timeline, you can write down your action items, like your demo, POC, customer case studies, proposal, etc. On the client's side, you can write down the customer's to-do list, which includes meeting with the Economic Buyer, detailed pain points, or formalized Decision Criteria. You may get something like this:

Make sure that unlike the above picture, actions happen on both sides to ensure a balanced process. There needs to be a to-do list on both the buyer's and seller's timeline. If you simply focus on accepting all the client's requirements without requesting any action from the client, you create a bad habit that will continue onwards without any constructive outcomes. You need to set out a process from day one to help create a mutually beneficial and balanced relationship.

You also need to look at the total timeline duration and try to shorten the sales cycle. After reworking the decision process with the client, rebalancing the tasks on both sides, and shortening the sales cycle, you may get a Decision Process that looks more like the image below, with more tasks on the client side and the total timeline reduced to 90 days instead of the initial 270 days (see how to do this below, under "Compelling Event").

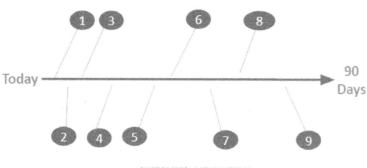

Paper Process

The paper process is the subset of the decision process dealing with the formal administrative process of a purchase order or a contract through the customer's Procurement and Legal departments. You will need to ask for the administrative approval process. Sometimes, a project manager who is your main contact and even your champion may not be clear about the process, especially if it is not a well-documented procedure or properly communicated internally. You will need to be proactive and ask for the process yourself. You can directly ask for the paper process. You could simply ask, "Can you tell me what exactly and practically has to happen for your organization to place the purchase order?"

They may not outline the entire process; they may just tell you that you need to have a meeting with the Director of Purchasing. So you inquire further:

"And then what happens?"

"Then it goes to Legal, who will review the terms of the agreement or the vendor's terms of services."

You continue with the same question: "And then what happens?"

When they respond, you follow up by again asking, "And then what happens?"

As you can see, you need to continue asking this question until the entire process has been laid out step by step. The mechanics of the paper process is not something you can change. It is something that's perfectly in place, well known by the Admin & Finance departments, but not always well known by the people you are dealing with at the beginning of the process. You need to make sure the answers you receive make sense and are in line with what you experience with other customers in the same industry. Once you have this process, you will have a clearer idea of what needs to be done to successfully close the sale. You will be able to plan this phase of the process and take it into account for forecasting purposes. Also, in most cases you can anticipate and perform some tasks in parallel instead of sequentially. For instance, you can share your Terms of Services with the legal department ahead of time to detect any issues and remedy them.

Compelling Event

One key concept that allows you to understand the timeline of an opportunity is the Compelling Event. *It is a deadline resulting from a business pressure, as perceived by the Economic Buyer, for making the purchasing/contracting decision.* It can be, for instance, the date of the end of maintenance of the incumbent solution, pushing your client to look for a replacement system before the incumbent stops the support. It could be the date when a new standard or regulation is enforced by authorities when the customer is obliged to perform certain tasks needing your product/service (like for the GDPR example mentioned above). It could be a promise made to the shareholders or a plan decided by the board to execute something.

The Compelling Event is the Economic Buyer's answer to the "Why Now?" question.

Unlike what some sellers think, your "end of quarter" or "end of the year" deadlines are not Compelling Events. They may be Compelling Events for you, but they are definitely not for the buyer. Obviously, one of the biggest challenges in closing a deal in a given timeframe and delivering on your forecast is finding the Compelling Event. We find the Compelling Event by asking ourselves, asking the champion, and ultimately asking the Economic Buyer: "Why Now?" If there is no strong and obvious answer, and if you can't find a Compelling Event for your opportunity, then you need to develop your metrics into the ROI and create the economic pressure of "missed revenue" or "missed savings" that would result from not buying now. We'll discuss this in more detail in the ROI chapter.

Chapter *SEVEN*

IDENTIFY PAIN

Pain is the core problem that you are trying to resolve for a prospect, and it is driving their interactions with you. A successful sales representative needs to be able to successfully identify pain and present their solution in a way that directly addresses that pain. In your sales process, the sooner you can identify this pain, the higher your chances of qualifying a prospect. There are multiple ways of identifying pains; from researching the business to asking the right questions and categorizing the pain identification process, everything needs to be given due diligence to successfully identify the pain and then to implement the targeted solutions.

Types of Pain

Pain could be of two different kinds. It could be a business problem within the account: for instance, the cost of operation is higher than the yield. These are business pains. The pain could also be related to a lack of capabilities: things that the customer can't satisfy for their own clients, for instance. The best pains are those that involve both. When a pain addresses both the capabilities and business, it becomes crucial!

How to Identify the Pain?

The simple answer is by asking the right questions in the right way.

Again, the T.H.E.D technique would work.

- "Tell me about your existing process of..."
- "How is xyz working today?
- "Explain to me..."
- "Describe to me the ..."

These types of open-ended questions help initiate a conversation that leads to a description of the pain. During these questions, whenever you feel that the prospect has touched upon a possible pain, you could ask them to further elaborate on that point. Continue doing this until you get specific details about the pain.

Language is Important

You need to be very careful about the words that you use to create a better and more fruitful flow of communication with your prospect. Avoid using the word 'pain,' obviously. Also avoid similar words that would bring a negative atmosphere into the conversation such as 'tell me about your problem.?" "what needs to be fixed?" or "what is wrong with your business?"

Instead, put them into a positive perspective and use questions like "what are you trying to improve?" or "how are you trying to add more value to your business?"

A technique that I prefer to use is actually to even start by asking very positive questions about their present status, such as "What do you like about your existing system?" You will let the client proudly express their achievements. They love talking about things that work well. While they describe the good things about the existing situation, you should acknowledge those facts through encouraging comments such as "This is fantastic!" Don't worry: 99% of time, once that's explained, without you having to ask anything, the client will transition by themselves to what needs to be improved. They add "but..." and will move on to explain what is not working. This way of interacting creates trust and confidence, since it's the client who initiates the conversation about the pain, not you.

You could also do your research by trying to identify the pain before the first discovery meetings. You could go through the CEO's messages on the website, read the company's blog, check their annual report, or follow them on LinkedIn or other social networking platforms to get a good understanding of their operations and broadly just what is going on in the company during that time.

Goals and objectives are obviously always related to some pains. Elon Musk would not announce Tesla's profitability goals for 2020 in 2019 if the company had not had "profitability" as the number one pain for years. In 2020, Tim Cook would not present a future iPhone in the low end market if Apple's pain was not the low-end market share in number of units sold worldwide.

Once you have started the process of the pain identification with one or two possible pains, you need to understand the consequences, the desired outcome, and the timeline.

Consequence

What are the consequences if the pain is left unaddressed? This key question helps to analyze and understand the scope and the importance of the pain. It should reveal the impact of the non-decision.

Desired Outcome

You need to understand the desired result that a client is envisioning. What exactly is it that a prospect expects the outcome to be? What impact will a given solution have on the objectives? You need to understand what outcome your prospect is trying to gain. Are they trying to get ahead of their competition? How much are they trying to reduce production costs? How much do they need to increase productivity?

Urgency: Compelling Event

Another important factor for addressing pain is urgency. This addresses the timeline by which the customer requires a solution to remedy the pain. As discussed earlier, this is called a Compelling Event: the deadline for a company, and more precisely for the Economic Buyer, to address the pain. Your goal will be to identify the urgency and create a reverse timeline from that deadline to define the Decision Process.

Please note that the key element for identifying pain is to address needs and not wants. The pain has to come from a point of need rather than a want. If you spend time and effort on an opportunity that is based on some nice-to-have benefits and not essentials, there is a high chance that no Compelling Event is there and that the deal may get delayed quarter after quarter.

It will be your responsibility to map out the Compelling Events to best understand your prospect's pain. You will need to connect the dots for your prospect and let them see how your solution will address the urgency of their pain.

Get More Information about the Pain?

Most sales reps just take the information that they are given by the prospect to identify pain. For instance, a prospect may say, "We would like to reduce the team turnover by 15% by next year." Sure, this is the desired outcome that a business is trying to achieve, but it also includes targeted metrics as well as the urgency of the situation. But what is the Compelling Event? What is the pain that has driven the business to create this deadline? What are the consequences if this deadline is not achieved? Questions like these differentiate you from your competition. You need to conduct your due diligence to identify the root causes of the pain and how it is impacting the business. Some of these questions may challenge your client to further analyze some aspects around the pain. That's ok. They will ultimately appreciate that you have taught them something or that you have challenged them to find answers to some questions that they have not been asking themselves. Most of the time, this relates to middle management and not the Economic Buyer. The EB usually has a perfect understanding of the why of the pain, the consequence of non-decision, and the expected outcome.

The MEDDIC Questions

To effectively ask questions, you will need to start by asking general questions at the beginning and then move on to more specific ones as you progress further through your sales process.

Initially, you will need to ask subtle questions to build rapport. Then you need to focus on more tangible questions to build confidence; these questions need to help qualify a lead based on the MEDDIC methodology.

Once you have been able to build a relationship of trust, you could then move on to the more specific MEDDIC questions. These questions will help you to demonstrate ownership on both ends.

The Challenger Consultant

It is when the customer starts sharing their problems with you that you start building confidence. This is when you become more of a consultant rather than a sales rep. Your objective at this point is not to sell anything, but rather to create a relationship built on trust and mutual benefit. They need to feel that you understand the issues. By asking deeper questions based on your experience from other customers, you can challenge them further on the consequences, expected results, and timeline.

Once you have built a rapport with them, you will be able to earn the right to advance through the sales process. You can become the trusted advisor.

Chapter *EIGHT*

CHAMPION

The champion is someone that will drive customers to take action in your favor. It is the person that you have the best relationship with inside the account. He/she is the person that will make the sale for you even when you are not around. It could get very difficult to truly identify your prospect's pain, get access to the Economic Buyer and, understand the Decision Criteria that will give you the leverage to successfully close the deal. The champion helps you with all these matters.

There are some specific characteristics of a champion. These include:

- Understands, likes, and supports our solution.

- Sponsors your solution during internal meetings.

- Is reasonably powerful (not necessarily buying decision).

- Is respected in the company (technical, economic, business...) and has access to the Economic Buyer.

- Has his/her own personal goals and motivations.

- Uses us as a means to achieve his/her goals.

Access to the Economic Buyer

One of the key characteristics of the champion is that they have access to the Economic Buyer, the person with the decision power. In some cases, the champion could, in fact, be the Economic Buyer, the CIO, or the CMO of a company. But even if not, then he/she is the person who will have access to them.

Respect & Credibility

The champion needs to have good credibility within the company. They need to be a person of influence if not power. They need to have enough influence in the organization to influence decisions.

Favorable Relation with You

The champion needs to be your friend. They need to be willing to answer your questions, inform you about any changes that may be relevant to you, and be aligned with your interests. They need to assist your sales process and work with you towards successfully closing a sale.

Personal Win

This is oftentimes overlooked. But in my opinion, this is one of the most crucial aspects of creating a good relationship with a champion. They need to have something to win from this decision/project. All champions need to have a reason to want your solutions.

Champions are typically successful, young guys who are still progressing and being promoted. They are the ones wanting to be the guy who implements solutions that positively affect the organization. They want to be able to say, "I was the one who implemented the solution that solved the pain or achieved the metrics." In most strategic sales, champions are promoted after the implementation of solutions that yield desired gains. To find that champion, you need to find out more about the people in the organization who have previously implemented successful solutions and, as a result, were recently promoted.

The Champion Needs You to Win

A champion needs to be rooting for you! They need to be invested in your solution and WANT you to score the sale. Again, this will circle down to having personal gains from it. Oftentimes, reps overlook a few characteristics of a champion and mistake an informer, a coach, or a friend in the organization to be the champion. While all these people in the organization may have a good rapport with you, they aren't the champions because they aren't invested in your solutions. All these individuals only have a neutral relationship with you. They may assist you through the process, introduce you to the Economic Buyer, and may even encourage a sale. But they wouldn't always have a strong enough motive to take your sales through. A champion WILL be someone who needs to be on your side and support your solution like their own because he/she has something to gain from it. A champion may not seem too friendly or have a great relationship with you, but, profoundly, they would want you to win.

Champions vs. Coaches

This is another common misconception: coaches are mistaken for champions. A champion is your internal sales rep. A champion is a person standing up for your solution! Say there is a room full of people, and one says, "We don't want to be purchasing a solution from a specific buyer (you). Does anyone have a problem with that?"

Your champion is the person who would raise their hand and say "Me. I have a problem with this suggestion. It will be a wrong decision to eliminate this vendor because of xyz."

That is the true definition of a champion. He or she is the one standing up in the accounts for you. They are the ones fighting for your business. They are your champion!

It takes time to identify, build, and nurture a champion. Both of you need to work hand in hand for each other's interests. They are the ones who will call you up the moment they hear news of their organization leaning towards your competition so that you can prepare to gain leverage. They are the ones who can give you an advantage over your competition.

On the other hand, a coach is a guide. A coach may or may not have the power of decision and doesn't necessarily want or need your solutions. Also, a coach most likely doesn't have anything to gain from supporting you. So they may be favorable to you, but they don't have the motivation to drive your sales through for you. All these characteristics can make the coach feel like a champion because they truly are friendly. But their position is not strong enough for them to become a champion.

The following table summarizes the differences between the champion, coach, and Economic Buyer.

Champion Qualification Table

	SYMPATHY TO US	POWER TO RECOMMEND	POWER TO BUY	PERSONAL GOAL
Champion	✓	✓	May be	✓
Coach/Friend	✓	May be	May be	May be
Economic Buyer	May be	May be	✓	May be

Why Do You Need a Champion?

The fact is you NEED a champion to sell. No sales happen without a champion. It really is as simple as that. You need a person that the organization trusts, and you need that person to trust YOU in order to increase your chances of making a sale.

A champion with a powerful and strong standing in the organization can greatly help shorten your sales cycle. Your champion will inform you of the challenges during the sales process well in advance, giving you the opportunity to fix issues. Since you have already established trust with the champion, it's easier and faster to influence the rest of the organization.

They may also be able to help enlarge the scope of the opportunity and help you close a bigger deal. For instance, in multi-year SaaS contracts, they can help you sign a longer term. Having a champion means the entire organization is more open to your solutions and will be willing to do more business than they had initially planned.

A champion will also become your go-to person to test your strategy during the sales campaign. They can assist you regarding what will and what may not work for their organization to help you tweak your offering or your sales strategy for higher chances of successfully closing the deal.

Could There Be More Than One Champion?

A champion is anyone who is working for the interests of your business; hence there could be as many as you can help nurture and build a great rapport with.

In big and strategic accounts, there is a fair chance you will require more than one champion to assist you through the process. You can have champions on the technical side and also on the business side. A champion on the technical side can help during the validation process and influence the Economic Buyer regarding decisions related to endorsing technology. On the other hand, a business champion will help leverage the technical champion's suggestions and help during the approval process. If anything, having more than one champion would further strengthen your chances of making a sale. You could have more than two champions too, depending on the 'pain' that you are focusing on and the scope of the opportunity. These could include a champion in the IT department, another in Marketing, and one in Procurement.

Why Do You Need a Champion?

Why would you even want to nurture a champion when you can use your own sales prowess to sell your solution? The fact is you are not informed of the real interactions, the power base, inside politics, and different stakeholders' motivations inside the account. Moreover, an organization will trust their own people more than they'd trust anything that you'd have to say. So, you could be saying that you offer "the best solution in the world with proof," and it wouldn't be good enough. A champion could say something around the lines of, "I trust these guys and their solutions." And it would be all an Economic Buyer would need to hear to drive the decision in your favor.

A champion helps open doors. A champion will be your go-to person every time you have a problem in the account. A champion can help in all the steps of their decision process. Say you are going through a Proof of Concept, but you have a few concerns. All you need to do is approach your champion and ask them for guidance.

How to Know if You Have a True Champion?

What if the champion doesn't provide you with all the necessary details? There is a fair chance that someone might be pretending to be your champion, but they are not acting as a champion behind closed doors.

You should always be qualifying the champion! Are they sending you unsolicited information about key news that will have an impact on the opportunity? Do they spontaneously call or email to inform you about a fact impacting the scope of the opportunity or the timeline? Are they replying to some of your informal questions where they don't HAVE TO reply but it would be NICE if they did? Do they reply to your after-hours emails?

A true champion would be able to provide you with valuable information regarding your concerns. They will be able to tell you if you are on the right track. And, if they don't, then they may not be the champion. Let's say you approach your champion with a concern, saying you aren't comfortable investing so much time and energy on this project since you don't believe you have a fair chance of scoring the deal. You announce them that you are considering to pull out of the deal. Your champion will be able to truthfully guide you if you do have a chance at it or how you need to build up your plans to improve your chances of scoring the deal. They will be able to tell you why you have a better chance of scoring the deal compared to your competition.

Or, if they begin avoiding the question or not providing valuable information that you seek, then there is a fair chance that they are not your champion!

What is the Value to the Customer for Having a Champion?

Champions are not just helpful to vendors. They are actually a crucial part of the decision and implementation process for their employers. They help to aptly convey the business's pains. They will be able to represent the company and its problems in a collaborative and constructive manner. They will know what the organization expects from a solution and will be able to direct you in the right direction.

A champion will be able to present opportunities for the organization to excel, advance, and grow. They will assist the implementation of your solution. Remember, their personal win is a successful implementation of the product/service. So, they play a key role in making that happen.

Building Champions

Now that we have established the definition, the importance, and the need for a champion, let's see how we can find and develop them.

There's a slim chance that a prospect would walk up to you in the hallway and introduce themselves as your champion. That is not going to happen. Champions are built over-time. Just like a sweet deal, they take time, effort, nurture, and, above all, specific characteristics, as described in the beginning of this chapter, to get to the point of becoming your champion.

You need to find someone whose interests align with yours and who has similar objectives in mind.

How to Identify Your Champion

Champions have very specific characteristics, which sometimes makes it difficult to identify them. For instance, someone who sympathizes with you could just be a coach. Someone who has the power to recommend or buy may just be the Economic Buyer. Primarily, you need to check a prospect against three main criteria to qualify them as a champion. These include someone who sympathizes, someone who has personal gain, and someone who has the credibility and the power to recommend. An additional criterion is for them to have the power to buy, but it is not necessary as long as they have access to the Economic Buyer and can influence their decision.

How to Find Champions BEFORE Demos

For this section, by "demo" I mean a customer
meeting, in the beginning of the sales process, where you both
discover the client's needs and make an initial standard brief
presentation.

A good idea is to research participants ahead of a
demo. Ideally, you should have a list of potential champions
handy before the demo to gain leverage and target your sales
strategies accordingly. The following are some characteristics
you need to look for.

Try to find people within the organization who have
been instrumental in implementing successful
products/services in the past. You want someone the
organization already trusts to make the right decisions,
someone with experience in purchasing the right deals. They
may or may not be in higher positions in the company, but
they have gained the trust of the organization with their
previous track record and gained respect and credibility.

You want someone passionate about their work and
their company and who talks about "the good of the company."
They will have a speech that will bring together different
stakeholders with divergent opinions. It is also these people
who know how to speak at the wavelength that the Economic
Buyer would understand and respect.

Seniority in the job and in the company: if there is a
potential champion who hasn't been in the company for long,

then you may want to try and get a better understanding of their standing in the business. Are they in a position of power and respect? Will they be heard? Will their opinions matter to the Economic Buyer? If yes, then you could run your screening checklist with them.

For older employees, as mentioned earlier, you want to focus more on their track record rather than on their position. A person in a strong position in the company in terms of title may not be very respected if they have made multiple bad calls or aren't too enthusiastic about integrating newer software or processes. They may hold a strong position, but they may not be a strong contender to become your champion. Someone who has stayed in the same position for a very long period of time may not have the mindset of bringing change. They may not even have any personal goals or ambition that could be linked to the success of the opportunity.

How to Find Champions DURING Demos

Keep looking for champions during demos. This is the perfect time to assess how they respond to your solution. The following are some indicators to help screen your prospects.

The ones asking questions: look for people who bring up real problems related to the pain, people who would ask questions and request explanations and examples. They will be the ones who are completely invested in your demos and maintain eye contact. Their questions are pertinent to the pain and not about the irrelevant details.

If the meeting is in-person and not virtual, there is a high chance your future champion is sitting by the #1 person in the room if they are not that person themselves. They act as a facilitator, if not a leader, seeking questions from other participants to make sure everyone is involved. If someone they consider unimportant asks too many questions or intervenes, they will shorten their questions and help you to move on. Similarly, if they feel someone important has been silent, they seek their engagement and ask them questions to get a sense of where they stand.

This person will listen to you when you talk. Even if they challenge you with some tough questions, their line of questioning would be a valid concern, relevant and legitimate. Their questions have positive notions to them and will be justified. As a sales rep, you would welcome those questions, as they should allow you to further explain the features and leverage the true value of your solution.

How to Connect with Champions AFTER Demos

Once you have established a pathway for communication through your demo, you could then strengthen this bond by finding commonalities between the two of you. Look for the person's background all the way back to high school. Do you share similar interests, clubs, family background, or basically anything that would help create a connection? People bond with people they have associations with much more easily; it makes them feel they belong to the same "group".

Ask them questions about their job, their professional and personal goals, their thoughts on this opportunity, and the way it will impact their job in the short term and the long term. The main idea is to continue communicating with them and adding a personal level to the communication channel. You need to regularly communicate with them to go beyond the pure formal relationship. You may want to share some personal information about yourself in your one-to-one communication to help establishing the connection. That could be about your career, why you joined this vendor, and your career goals.

Don't be 'salesy'. The idea is to establish trust via healthy channels of communication. Ideally, you should be communicating with them regularly; depending on the scope of the deal, this could be as frequent as daily. It doesn't necessarily have to be a long call every morning, but just an informational e-mail, a short text message, or a quick call a few times each week will help establish a healthy communication channel for sharing and attaining information.

Test the Champion

A lot of people in the organization would like to have a good rapport with you, but they may not always have your interests in mind, the inclination to help you, or even the authority to provide the solutions that you may require from them. Hence, you must test the champion to see if they will pull through on their promises. You need to test them against the definition that we established earlier in this chapter.

The following are a few ways to test a champion's allegiance.

Is the person able to provide insider information? This doesn't have to be company secrets or confidential information, just information that wouldn't otherwise be immediately available to the general public on their website, some insider information to help you in different phases of the sales process. One of the best examples is an organization chart. Nowadays, org charts can be figured out through the web and professional social networks such as LinkedIn. So, an org chart is not really confidential information, but most companies don't publish their org chart. Asking the champion to share the org chart is a good test.

The champion should be comfortable sharing information regarding the company's long and short term goals and other key objectives that may help you to represent your solution in a more targeted manner. Ask them about the key pain that keeps the Economic Buyer awake at night.

In a later phase, your champion should be able to validate your metrics and your ROI pitch (Return on Investment). They should be able to give feedback about how the Economic Buyer could perceive your ROI pitch.

Your champion needs to have enough authority to help set up meetings with the Economic Buyer or other authoritative persons in the organization. Asking them to organize such meetings is a great test to know if they are the champions you think they are.

There are three main why's they need to answer:

- Why buy at all?
- Why buy from us?
- Why buy now?

Test the champion by asking these questions to see if he/she has the maturity for the role. This is also possibly something the Economic Buyer will ask them, directly or indirectly, sooner or later in their buying process. They had better know the answer if they are supposed to be the one who sells in the account on your behalf.

How does your solution help accomplish personal goals for the champion? They should have a pretty solid, meaningful, and mutually beneficial answer to this question to be eligible for the position.

Finally, after you have established a rapport with them, one of the best ways to test your champion, and at the same time set expectations, is to ask them directly, "If, towards the end of my quarter, this project has not closed yet, and I need your help to push inside to get the contract signed, will you help me?" In other words, if you wonder if they are your champion, ask them.

Chapter NINE

THE ROI PITCH

Return on Investment is a very important aspect of the sales process; your prospect needs to know the value that they are getting with your solution. This is why Metrics is a key element of MEDDIC.

When training sales teams on MEDDIC, I observe that most salespeople don't act on the METRICS that they obtain from the prospect. They are not leveraging the power of the METRICS into a nice, easy, convincing, pertinent ROI story.

Metrics without ROI is as useless as knowledge without action. It's like measuring your body fat, becoming aware that you're overweight, and then doing nothing about it.

You need to show how metrics translate into dollars. Either they help to increase revenue/income, or they contribute to decreasing costs. The whole purpose of METRICS within the MEDDIC methodology is to show the economic impact of your solution.

You need to have a process that will transform your METRICS, almost automatically, into monetary SAVINGS or GAINS. Because that's what the economic buyer is interested in. That's the reason why the customer buys your solution to start with. And that process is that we are going to cover here.

ROI vs. Payback Period

First, I prefer talking about the PAYBACK PERIOD instead of RETURN ON INVESTMENT. Payback sounds easier on the ear and provides a clearly quantifiable gain for non-financial people in the organization. A real ROI analysis is expressed in percentage. It sounds too financial, can be complex, and is hard to elaborate. It may actually be difficult for non-financial salesperson to build it. It can be even harder for the non-financial people at your client to understand.

Unlike the ROI, Payback Period is expressed in time(years or, hopefully, months). It's easier to quickly calculate and present. It's also easier to visualize and understand. It's not easy to understand what having a ROI of x% instead of y% represents or means for the company or for the EB's budget. However, anyone understands what getting one's money back within x months means. When simulating the Payback Period of an investment for your client, the intent would be the same as an ROI pitch, but it would be in a simpler language.

Here are the definitions of the ROI and the Payback Period.

$$ROI = \frac{(Gain\ from\ Investment - Cost\ of\ Investment)}{Cost\ of\ Investment}$$

$$\text{Payback Period} = \frac{\text{COST of Investment}}{\text{Annual Profit}}$$

Let's pick an example. Let's say a business implemented solution A to divide engineering cycles by half. They need six months to design their products with your solution, versus twelve months for the incumbent solution or with the competition.

- The cost of your solution: $200k
- The size of the team: 10 engineers
- Annual cost of an engineer: $80k, including overhead
- Annual cost of the team: $800k
- Annual savings: $400k
- Profit: $200k ($400k-$200k)
- Example 1 Payback: 200/400= 0.5 years
- Example 1: ROI: 400/200= 200%
- ROI: 200%
- Payback: 6 months

This is a pretty simple pitch that provides all the information that a business needs to understand the gains from your solution. You or your prospect don't need to be a CFO to understand this.

As you may have noticed, there is no conversation about the pricing, but rather it is on the gains. A prospect will not visualize the cost of your solution, but they will see the returns that it will generate. It doesn't matter if the prospect thinks your solution is 'too expensive.' All they will focus on is how it will benefit them.

> ***You sell when you move the conversation from COST to VALUE.***

You are also creating urgency in the account. You prove how, by not implementing solution, they are 'throwing money out the window.' This is a really powerful message for your customer. Of course, you'll need more details in your presentations for the Economic Buyer or the CFO; it will need to include all the nitty gritty details. But, for a quick view of what your solution can do for a prospect's business, this is a perfect representation.

Based on the above example, each day delaying the PO (Purchase Order) will cost them over $1000. "Mr. customer, since our conversation last week, you just lost $7000 as we talk and don't implement." That's $1000 down the drain every single day for not implementing your solution!

This diffuses the requests for discounts because the prospect is more focused on the gains rather than the cost of the solution.

Your solution could actually be 50% more expensive, and they would still want it. In that case, the Payback Period would be 9 months instead of 6. They would still be losing over $500 every single day by not buying and not implementing your solution.

The Process to Pitch the Payback Period

Calculations don't have to be complex or difficult to understand. Basic calculations that mainly highlight the returns for a prospect are more than enough to get your point across. Have a process in place to speak about your Payback Period. Doing so would help to keep matters on track and to quickly help you move forward to the closing. Use a white board when possible to interactively calculate it with them. The impact is much higher.

The process should begin by expressing the METRICs. Move on to quickly estimating the monetary gains from your solution, either in the form of increased revenue or reduced costs. Then move on to calculating the cost of your solution and the estimates costs of its implementation as well as other indirect costs. Finally, talk about the Payback Period in several months just as we did in the example above.

The Benefit of the Quick ROI Approach through the Payback Period

The following are just some of the many benefits that this quick ROI approach or Payback Period can have on your sales process.

- It helps create urgency. You let the client know how they are losing money every passing minute by not implementing your solution.

- When you are desperately looking for a Compelling Event, the urgency created is a great alternative to the Compelling Event. They need to buy urgently.

- It allows you to avoid the conversation around pricing. Since the client's focus is directed towards the value your solution is brining, it doesn't even make sense to ask for discounts. You could sell at a higher price and still present a value to them.

- It gives confidence to your non-financial people, and it typically pumps up your champion to take you to the EB. People who aren't directly in tune with the finances of their organization will get a better understanding of your solution, which will help them in getting the internal approval The champion feels confident that you know how to talk to the EB.

- It helps you speak at the same frequency as the Economic Buyer. You will have a very clear and upfront conversation with them. It will trigger any objection they may have. You can know them and handle them.

As you can see there is a huge value in articulating simply the Payback Period in a sharp and short way. The method we covered here applies to any situation with metrics (as per the definition we gave). Practice it for yourself in past deals and make it a habit for future opportunities.

CHAPTER *TEN*

SAY NO TO QUALIFY AND TO CLOSE

Saying no is very important in every business journey. It is a tool and accessory that is strategically and effectively used by the most successful salespeople. As a sales rep, you need to understand why you need to say no, when the right time to say no is, and what is the best way to say it.

There are two main areas where it is important to be able to say no: during the qualification phase and during the closing phase. You may need to say no during the qualification phase to better understand what the client needs. It will also help to test whether the customer is the right fit for your solution. During the closing, saying no helps accelerate the sales process.

We want to qualify and assess prospects efficiently by trying to evaluate deals promptly. This helps in determining if the prospect will end up buying from you, and, further, if they will become successful users of your products. The best sellers are the ones that are the best at qualification. The most successful sales reps are the ones who make the best judgments regarding their prospects.

Why Say No?

Saying no is not natural, so much so that it seems much easier to just say yes to please the prospects. Saying yes seems like the 'nice' thing to do. This is because, by saying no, we often feel that we're hurting the recipient of this response. Although it's not natural, saying no is an efficient way to success.

The most common elements of MEDDIC where we might say no are the Decision Criteria and the Decision Process. In the Decision Criteria, saying no helps us to assess those criteria, and it also helps us to focus on the essential elements.

It's also important when the prospect has a "wrong" criterion in their Decision Criteria. It could be a feature that no other customer is asking for, that we don't offer, and that the competitor is offering. It could be a criterion in the zone that we earlier called the Danger Zone. It's better to say no to this and explain why it's useless by referring to hundreds of clients who are successfully using the solution without this criterion. If they agree that it is not essential, and they remove it from their Decision Criteria, we have managed to flatten the playing field or even tilt it in our favor. It they don't, there is a high chance we'll lose the deal because we are not fulfilling this request—and, most importantly because of the hidden reasons why that criterion is even listed and why they disagree to remove it.

Similarly, we also say no in the Decision Process, as it is a great way to remove unnecessary activities. If we can manage to say no to one of their long and irrelevant activities that they are presenting, and if they agree to remove it, then we'll shorten the Decision Process.

You will, of course, need to be very thorough with your explanation of why you are saying no and why it is not essential for their business. You need to explain why their industry never asks for those features because they don't influence the bottom line. Once you have focused on the positives and given them all the reasons why they shouldn't be focusing too much on this one criterion, you need to let them decide the outcome. If they still aren't convinced, if they still think that that feature is essential for their business, then you may need to walk away from that account.

On the contrary, if they agree with you and are willing to overlook that feature, then kudos to you! You have managed to adjust the Decision Process, possibly shortening the sales process.

Generally, saying no has many other benefits. Human psychology doesn't like a yes man. We are rarely attracted to someone who keeps saying yes to everything because they eventually lose their credibility.

Even in personal relationships between two partners, one may say yes to everything. With this behavior, a person would seem like a desperate seller, and buyers do not like buying from desperate sellers. You want to get closer to the "trusted advisor" role, which is achieved by creating credibility, done by saying no at appropriate times.

Other Benefits of Saying No

Another psychologically important factor of saying no is that when you do it after saying yes at several times, you automatically increase your credibility for those yeses from before. It makes the yeses more valuable, and they instantly feel more real and more credible. Because, unconsciously, your ability to say no shows that those yeses were true. And this is one of the foolproof ways of becoming a trusted advisor.

By saying no, you move away from that yes man type of a seller, a desperate seller, to the trusted advisor role.

How to Say No During Closing

Let's talk about the most exciting way to say no:, during closing. Many salespeople are scared to say no during closing, and that's one of the reasons why sales get delayed from one quarter to another. It is important to make sure to be confident about your deal by saying no in the closing, and that's MEDDIC. If the elements of MEDDIC are solidly checked, with a strong champion backing you and an EB sponsoring it and everything else checked, you should feel confident and use the NO to accelerate the sales. Saying no during the closing phase may seem like risk taking, but it actually turns out more beneficial.

Most importantly, saying no during closing removes unnecessary steps during the closing. It forces the prospects to think if that last minute requirement is even that necessary. As a result, it would shorten the sale cycle and get you that purchasing order.

Your NO should be said nicely. Always be courteous and pleasant, even when you disagree. Your NO should also always be accompanied by a reason. Without a reason, your NO would just seem stubborn and without insight.

Also, always focus back on the positives when you say NO. Don't linger on the negatives for too long. As mentioned in the previous chapter, your sales strategy should focus on how to convince them that by not implementing your solution, their business is losing money by the second! This is what you should be redirecting your focus on after every NO. You need to continue reinforcing the positive values of your solution. You also should focus back on the pain and how your solution can help to instantly eliminate it.

Examples

Say you are coming towards the end of the quarter and are about to receive the PO, but the Head of Procurement informs you that they would like to negotiate the terms of the contract. These could be payment terms, licensing, verbiage, etc. Your answer should be around the lines of, "I wish I could help, but I am so sorry I absolutely can't. We are a public company and, by modifying these terms, we'd be publicly reported, and we absolutely cannot risk doing that."

This answer shows respect for their query but provides a firm no as an answer with a solid reason for doing so.

Another great answer for similar query could be, "We are regularly audited, and going beyond these terms requires a special statement from the CFO, and I cannot do that. Even if I did, it would take over three to four weeks to get the process going. Is it really important to go through all that time-consuming hassle to simply revise the contract from 30 days to 60 days? Is it really worth it to let your business suffer a loss of $3000 per day by causing unnecessary delays? How would the EB feel if you tell them that you are delaying the purchase for a month? Imagine postponing the contract by 30 days which could cost well over $90,000 (30 days by $3000). Is your Economic Buyer ready to suffer a six figure loss just because you want to change a few wordings and requirements in the contract?"

As you can see, you can use metrics and the power of the EB and your champion to intervene.

CHAPTER *ELEVEN*

MEDDIC vs. BANT

During a recent Sales Kickoff, as we reviewed qualification criteria from the sales rep's perspective, one rep asked a question about BUDGET. It reminded me of my very first sales qualification method that I learned in the 80s, BANT. This book would be incomplete without talking about BANT.

BANT is one of the oldest sales qualification checklists, which seems to make a lot of sense.

1. BUDGET
2. AUTHORITY
3. NEEDS
4. TIMING

These are typically the things that you want to check before spending time with a prospect, one may say. I consider them to still be valid if you are both in an inbound call situation AND if you are in a simple sales process, typically transaction sales, with a very short sales cycle. In other words, if someone calls you, wants to buy your product, and asks for a small effort, such as a short demo or a quick quote, then you should ask those four BANT questions and, if all is good, you deliver what they ask and quickly move to the closing phase. In all other cases, BANT should be BANNED!

Here's why:

Budget should not be a sales criterion of qualification.

Why? Because of Metrics, the M of MEDDIC. If you have Metrics, or if you can obtain and document them, then since you know how to transform it into ROI and take it to the EB, you don't need any budget prior to your work. The EB will redefine priorities to get the economic benefit ASAP. Remember, as discussed in the ROI chapter above, buying from you becomes an act of saving costs or revenue boosting. Since when does an EB need to have budgeted anything to save money or to increase revenue? The beauty of MEDDIC is that it transforms the urgency of sales into urgency from the prospect to buy in order to save costs or to increase revenue. You don't need to have a budget for any of these. Any EB is able to prioritize expenditures so that they can achieve and observe those savings ASAP.

Neither should Timing

Since the MEDDIC approach creates urgency thanks to the economic impact, even a non-scheduled purchase becomes possible. So, timing should not be a qualification criterion either. A convinced EB will always accelerate a project, for their own benefit, to start seeing gains sooner.

BANT used to be popular. It does not work anymore. It was actually never aggressive enough for any company offering a product or service that brings measurable gains. The success of MEDDIC proves that neither the budget nor the timing should be in your qualification criteria. Also, MEDDIC proves that there is a lot more to Sales Qualification than just the NEED (which is the "I" of MEDDIC or Identify Pain) and the AUTHORITY (which is the E of MEDDIC or the Economic Buyer). Existence of Metrics, the knowledge of Decision Criteria and the Decision Process, the existence of a Champion, and the understanding of the Competition represent a lot of things to consider in order to fully qualify an opportunity.

Since budgets are typically annual, when they exist it means that a pain has been expressed at least a year ago, decision criteria have been defined, and sometimes even an RFP has been written. Experience shows that your chances of qualifying such a deal or winning it are always much lower than when you get into an account sooner, identify pain, get metrics, help write decision criteria, and sell without a preexisting budget.

As an example, all the four letters of BANT can be checked, but you may still easily lose the deal when the RFP is written under your competitor's influence and the decision criteria are not in your favor (Decision Criteria). In another case, you will most definitely lose a deal even of all four elements of BANT are solidly checked but your competition has a strong champion and not you (Champion). I can keep going with examples involving the EB or DP. These are the reasons why BANT is incomplete, wrong and can be misleading. You would disqualify opportunities who may be closed while wasting time on those which have no chance of closing.

CONCLUSION

I hope you liked this book.

> We are what we repeatedly do. Excellence, then, is not an act but a habit.

*Actually By Will Durant based on Aristotle's ideas

~ Aristotle

Next is to put all the above into practice. Like every lesson we learn in our personal or professional life, only practice allows the lesson to become a habit. Here are other action items for you to develop your sales qualification skills:
- Take self-paced courses online
  https://trainings.meddic.academy/

- Join an upcoming vILT (Virtual Instructor-Led Training) at https://meddic.academy/vilt-virtual-meddic-workshops/ or directly here.
- If you are a sales manager, make sure you check out our Managers courses and programs at https://meddic.academy/

WILL YOU DO ME A FAVOR?

If you enjoyed the book ALWAYS BE QUALIFYING, would you mind taking a minute to write a review on Amazon? Even a short review helps, and it means a lot to me.

If your team members, your colleagues or any friend you care about is in sales, please send them this link :

https://meddic.academy/always-be-qualifying-meddic-the-book/

Finally, if you'd like to stay in touch with me, connect with me on LinkedIn by using my email: darius@meddic.academy

ALWAYS BE QUALIFYING :-)

ACKNOWLEDGEMENTS

Thanks to Steve Walske for his out-of-the-box leadership. Steve was the CEO of PTC and loved being involved in sales, in sales meetings, and customer meetings. He was the business genius behind the existence and growth of PTC. During his tenure, the company had over 40 quarters of consecutive double or triple digit growth as a public company. Here's one anecdote which shows how extraordinary he is: during a management meeting in Berlin in 1993, with half of the company's sales managers present, he stopped me on a slide in which I was showing the triple digit growth of my per-sales-rep "productivity", (i.e. growth with the same headcount), consistently quarter after quarter, and used it as an example to follow for all other managers. Of course he promoted me, on the spot, and didn't care about any protocol. That promotion led to France beating Dassault in its own fiefdom one year later. Steve used to make smart and right decisions very fast.

Thanks to Mike Mc Guinness for his unique personality. Mike is a rare kind of sales leader who knows how to mix empathy, honesty and aggressive sales leadership to achieve success in a desirable human environment. He also delivered the best part of the sales training I received at PTC during my own on-boarding when I joined the company as an early sales manager. Mike's content was sharp, process oriented, articulate, and practical. In my view, it was the foundation of what later became MEDDIC. He was then the VP of Sales, US at PTC. I used and reused Mike's "Formula for Success" for years. It was in the form of a one pager, summarizing the quantified sales activity a rep needed to have in order to achieve quota. That page hung on all my reps' walls during my tenure at PTC. Years later, although I was never a direct report, he interrupted his Tokyo-Boston flight with a stop in Paris when he learned about my resignation to understand why I was leaving and to see if there was a way I could stay. His values of humility and integrity set him aside from everyone else.

Thanks to John Mc Mahon for hiring me at PTC. Everyone in the industry knows he is a legend, so I am just going to share an anecdote related to his ability to sell as a hiring manager. I was introduced by a German headhunter, and we met at Hotel Intercontinental in Paris in December 1991. In that first interview, he managed to basically tell me that despite they had failed in the recruitment of the position for which I was interviewed (Country Manager France) three times in the preceding two years, and that all those three former managers were still in the organization, demoted somewhere but kept their original titles, because they couldn't fire them or demote them officially due to the French labor laws, in a way that I thought I was getting the easiest job possible. It's hilarious when I think back. His charismatic leadership and the strength of his character were instrumental for attracting me and many others to PTC, and later in the companies he has been advising.

Thanks to Scott Rudy for his mentorship and vision. I got to know Scott at Think3 where we doubled down the same hyper growth experience that we had at PTC, for a few years. I am grateful he called me in 2004 to join him there. Thanks to Scott's support and coaching I had a blast applying MEDDIC and transforming the declining organization in Western Europe into a team three times bigger with four times more revenue and profit, two years later. Scott is an example of smart and ethical sales leadership.

I could keep going with a large number of friends, family and clients who encouraged and helped me in writing this book to whom I am grateful.

I am just going to close my acknowledgements with special thanks to Goran Malmberg, CEO of Mentice, also a sales leader at PTC in the early days, as well as Kris Thyregod VP EMEA at Silver Peak, both great MEDDIC Academy clients, for providing insight and feedback as I was finalizing this book.

This was,

ALWAYS BE CLOSING

MEDDIC

Edition 5 – July 2020

ISBN: 978-0-9892957-6-5

Made in the USA
Coppell, TX
23 February 2022

74000941R00085